R O B E R T   B U G H

when the bottom drops out

finding grace in the depths of disappointment

Tyndale House Publishers, Inc.
Carol Stream, Illinois

Visit Tyndale online at www.tyndale.com.

TYNDALE and Tyndale's quill logo are registered trademarks of Tyndale House Publishers, Inc.

When the Bottom Drops Out: Finding Grace in the Depths of Disappointment

Copyright © 2011 by Robert Bugh. All rights reserved.

Cover illustration of scroll pattern copyright © by Christina Rodriguez/iStockphoto. All rights reserved.

Cover photograph copyright © PM Images/Photodisc/Getty Images. All rights reserved.

Wedding photo on page 211 copyright © élan Photography. Used with permission.

Author photo by Jon Langham copyright © 2011 by Wheaton Bible Church. All rights reserved.

Designed by Stephen Vosloo

All Scripture quotations, unless otherwise indicated, are taken from the Holy Bible, *New International Version,*® *NIV.*® Copyright © 1973, 1978, 1984 by Biblica, Inc.™ Used by permission of Zondervan. All rights reserved worldwide. www.zondervan.com.

Scripture quotations marked NLT are taken from the *Holy Bible*, New Living Translation, copyright © 1996, 2004, 2007 by Tyndale House Foundation. Used by permission of Tyndale House Publishers, Inc., Carol Stream, Illinois 60188. All rights reserved.

Scripture quotations marked ESV are taken from *The Holy Bible*, English Standard Version® (ESV®), copyright © 2001 by Crossway, a publishing ministry of Good News Publishers. Used by permission. All rights reserved.

Library of Congress Cataloging-in-Publication Data

Bugh, Robert.
    When the bottom drops out : finding grace in the depths of disappointment / Robert Bugh.
        p. cm.
    Includes bibliographical references (p.   ).
    ISBN 978-1-4143-6349-3 (sc)
    1. Suffering—Religious aspects—Christianity. 2. Grief—Religious aspects—Christianity. 3. Disappointment—Religious aspects—Christianity. 4. Consolation. 5. Bugh, Robert. I. Title.
    BV4909.B85 2011
    248.8'6—dc23   2011024187

Printed in the United States of America

18 17 16 15 14 13 12
 8   7   6   5   4   3   2

As we write these words, I (Larry) am less than a month away from cancer surgery. *When the Bottom Drops Out* reached deep places within us as few books have, arousing us to more firmly trust God, more givingly love each other, and more resolutely serve Christ's Kingdom. Can any impact be greater? Thanks, Rob!

LARRY CRABB, *Psychologist, founder of NewWay Ministries, author*
RACHAEL CRABB, *Author, board member of Greater Europe Mission*

Rob not only opens his heart, he shares how God entered into the story of his life in such a powerful way. Having suffered deep personal loss myself, I was profoundly stirred and blessed.

JERRY E. WHITE, *International president emeritus, The Navigators*

Follow the amazing journey one man took with God through trials that could have shattered his family and ended his ministry. Get ready to learn some life lessons as you discover how Rob Bugh pressed into God and found superhuman strength in Christ. Give a copy to your pastor or a seminary student too. The book's practical truth provides a gold mine of wisdom for life's tough roads.

TOM DOYLE, *Vice president and Middle East director for e3 Partners; author of* Breakthrough: The Return of Hope to the Middle East

Rob's account of his own plunge into the unknown is honest, engaging, and—most important—tested against the plumb line of Scripture. This is recommended reading for all of us, whether before, during, or after our own inevitable experiences of loss.

DUANE LITFIN, *President emeritus, Wheaton College*

When the Bottom Drops Out challenges some common misconceptions about life's difficulties. Because Pastor Bugh has been deeply wounded himself, he is able to communicate, with great sensitivity, the hidden *blessings* in suffering.

MARILYN HONTZ, *Author of* Shame Lifter *and* Listening for God

When the Bottom Drops Out touched me at points I've seldom experienced in literature. My pastor, Rob Bugh, does in print what I hear him do nearly every week. He grapples honestly with a real God who takes on all that is wrong in a pain-filled world. In this book, your mind will find guidance toward dealing with life's pains. Your heart will find hope.

LON ALLISON, *Executive director, Billy Graham Center, Wheaton College*

Rob has faced pain square in the eyes—lived in it, with it, and through it—and his story drips with authenticity, candor, and faith in a loving sovereign Creator who knows our afflictions. Thanks, Rob, for giving real help and sharing your story.

MICHAEL EASLEY, *Former president of Moody Bible Institute; lead pastor of Fellowship Bible Church, Nashville*

The depth of Rob's personal relationship to Jesus Christ, along with his deep conviction that God is sovereign, is eloquently shared in this remarkable book. Always returning to his rock-solid faith in the midst of terrible tragedies, Rob exemplifies the way people of faith should respond to crises.

HENRY L. DENEEN, *President, Greater Europe Mission*

With candor and passion, Rob explains how he immersed himself in "faith-work"—actively facing his pain, navigating through it, and embracing God's sovereignty in the midst of it. Rob richly layers his reflections with common sense and profound biblical expertise. This will be a must-read for my clients.

MARK MACDONALD, *Licensed Clinical Social Worker and owner of Mark MacDonald & Associates; coauthor of* Setting New Boundaries

In a time when people are embarrassed about their suffering and need help worshiping in their pain, Rob encourages us through first-person accounts, pastoral challenge, and biblical exposition. Here's water for dry hearts!

ANDREW J. SCHMUTZER, *Professor of biblical studies at Moody Bible Institute; author of* The Long Journey Home: Understanding and Ministering to the Sexually Abused

Rob Bugh gives to any of us who've ever been deeply disappointed with God a pathway to authentic faith and hope. I didn't want to put this book down. Then I wanted to give it to so many people I know.

DANIEL MEYER, *Senior pastor of Christ Church of Oak Brook (IL); host of Life Focus Television; author of* Leadership Essentials *and* Witness Essentials

When the Bottom Drops Out is an authentic and thought-provoking account of finding hope in the midst of great loss. The author also offers practical insight to healthy grieving during tragedy and obtaining abundant peace in great pain.

JENNIFER STENZEL, *Licensed Clinical Professional Counselor; executive director of Stenzel Clinical Services, Ltd.*

To my wife, Rhonda, and our seven children—Shannon, Nathan,

Kyle, Alissa, Kelly, Christine, and Ryan. The deaths of Rhonda's first

husband, Tom, and my first wife, Carol, have hit all nine of us hard,

but their faith and love continue to speak volumes, nowhere more so

than in your lives as you follow Jesus. I see them and Him in you.

Contents

Acknowledgments

THIS BOOK HAS been a family project. I have loved the input and corrections from our large family. Thanks, Rhonda, for the title. I appreciate all of you more than words can express.

In addition, I want to thank my tireless assistant, Donna Stone, who has worked and reworked this manuscript, all the while balancing everything else coming at me. You never complain.

Thanks, also, to the wonderful people at Tyndale—my close friend and mentor Chuck Stair, chairman of Tyndale's board; Jeff Johnson, COO, who is so passionate about the Kingdom; and Kim Miller, my gifted editor. All of you walked through my tragedy with me here at Wheaton Bible Church, and you have been an enormous help in getting my story into print. I am so grateful.

Thanks, finally to WBC—to the elders for giving me time off to write and always supporting me in hundreds of different ways; to the wonderful people of WBC who have prayed for and encouraged me—oh, how I value your love—and to our staff who are so competent and so committed. Last but not least, to my close friends here at WBC: you have been Jesus to me; few pastors have been so cared for. Thanks, Jeff, Jim, Dan, Brian, Chuck, Scott, Mark, Steve, and Mel.

Introduction

HAVE YOU EVER TRIED to convince yourself that if you believe enough and are godly enough, good things will happen—and if they do not, you'd better not let on so you don't appear less than spiritual?

That is nonsense. Every one of us experiences disappointment, difficulty, and adversity—the bottom falling out.

Of course, disappointment exists on a continuum. At one end are the minor irritations of life like "Why is this red light taking so long to change?" or "Why did the Cubs blow it again?" (I live in Chicago, am a Cubs fan, and know this isn't minor for some of you—sorry.) At the other end of the spectrum are the major life-altering, mind-numbing tragedies of tsunamis, divorce, and death.

As I write, the global recession continues to create significant economic and financial pain here in America and in many other countries. Retirement plans, not to mention dreams, have been shattered; jobs have been lost; entire markets, systems, and even countries have been destabilized. Yes, for some it has been just a minor irritation at one end of the continuum, but for many others this downturn has been a huge problem at the opposite end of the spectrum.

My burden is to help you develop a theology of disappointment, or better, a theology for handling disappointment (by theology I mean what we believe about God and life in His presence). My focus will be primarily on the major life-altering stuff because that's where I have lived and because the biblical principles that enable you to get through the greater issues apply equally to the lesser ones.

My point in this book will be simple: in Christ . . . you can do disappointment. You can handle discouragement, loss, and despair. I did, in spite of the fact that up until a few years ago I led a remarkably easy and comfortable suburban life.

What happened? First, my best friend, Tom, died; then a short time later my wife, Carol, died; and all this happened while the church I pastor in suburban Chicago was in the middle of a large and somewhat controversial relocation project (what relocation project isn't controversial?). In the midst of the most demanding period in my life, I experienced my greatest sorrow.

This is my story, but more important, it is the story of the amazing and sovereign grace of God in my life. I want to show you the supernatural Christ-centered peace He gave me in abundance, the way I've seen Him use tragedy to build His people, and the wonderful truths my heavenly Father has taught me in the darkness. It's really a story of the power of the gospel played out in one ordinary life.

Loss Can Be Horrific

However, there are two things I want to be clear about on the front end: I am not and will not be Pollyannaish about pain. My faith has never been about denial. Just the opposite. My tragedy was enormous; my loss, horrific. The bond between a husband and wife transcends all others. In a healthy marriage—and ours was—spouses do life, all of it, together. Nothing compares to the joy of a thriving marriage. So the loss death brings is total; the pain, pervasive. My nights at MD Anderson Cancer Center in Houston, sitting by my wife's bed and watching cancer leech her beautiful life out of her, were awful. Indescribably so.

Further, Tom, a leading surgeon in our area, and Carol were extraordinary people. That they were struck down in the prime of life (both were fifty) was mind-boggling. In spite of the prayers of God's people in many different parts of the world and the enormous amount of prayer taking place at our church, God did not choose to heal them. He promoted them. Our church, our two families, and especially our children were staggered by our losses. I have been and will continue to be transparent about the pain.

As a pastor, I've witnessed tremendous suffering in the lives of others as well. I've walked with parents reeling from the death of a child. Though the loss of a spouse severs the closest bond a person can have, the loss of a child results in perhaps the most acute pain one can experience. A child is your dependent; the one above all others whom you nurture.

Children should never precede parents in death, and when they do, it is numbing.

I've also seen firsthand the turmoil triggered by the Great Recession. In my first twenty-five years in the pastorate, I never counseled someone facing foreclosure. In the last several years, I've met with a number of families who were losing their homes.

I know that because of major losses like these, many of us, even committed Christ followers, are at times barely hanging on. The weight of our circumstances is just . . . well, crushing! (By the way, being a pastor makes one no more immune to suffering and confusion than being a soldier shields a person from enemy fire.) And when we deny our pain, we lose the opportunity to see Christ, to help others around us who are also suffering, and to point to Christ in the midst of our despair.

I choose not to do that.

God's Plan Involves Pain

On the other hand, and this is my second point, I believe God has a wonderful plan for our lives, but a plan that involves *pain*. Most important, God is sovereignly working His plan as He sees fit. He is in complete control of the universe and in complete control of our lives. God is not a distant supporting character but the central sovereign character in the unfolding drama of global redemption—one that He wills, initiates, and lovingly superintends from start to finish. This is His universe, His planet.

Life, ultimately, is not about us. Life is about God, His will, His ways, His purposes. No single biblical truth has been more foundational, more helpful to me than this: It's not my agenda that matters, it is God's. He is the master; I am His servant. So the psalmist declares, "The LORD has established his throne in heaven, and his kingdom rules over all" (Psalm 103:19). Job, believing this, amazingly embraces his devastating loss when he cries out, "The LORD gave and the LORD has taken away; may the name of the LORD be praised" (Job 1:21). And James, in the New Testament, assuming the sovereignty of God in good times and tough times, in effect tells us not to be surprised by adversity but to thrive in it. He writes, "Consider it pure joy, my brothers, whenever you face trials of many kinds, because you know that the testing of your faith develops perseverance" (James 1:2-3).

More on all this later, but I want to emphasize these two points now because if we minimize the pain and our disappointment because of the pain, we end up pretending, and we end up in image management. Though I don't know how it is where you live, over the years I have seen way too much image management among Christians.

However, if we fail to rest in the sovereignty of God, we have no rock, no foundation, no hope, and ultimately no answers. Worse, we have no spiritual spinal column (C. S. Lewis would say no *chest*). When disappointment and loss hit, we tend to lapse into self-pity or bitterness, questioning God and often consciously or unconsciously distancing ourselves from Him. We think, *If God loved me, how could He let this happen?* And my, do we complain, blame, lash out, and become angry or depressed!

Hear me: God has a plan for your life, but that plan involves pain—accept it! Be tough, be believing. Our goal, Christ followers, isn't to be comfortable or even to preserve our lives at all cost; our goal is to be faithful, to do hard things for Jesus Christ. Stated differently, I have learned to live with a tension that I think is key to spiritual health— on the one hand, pain is an ever-present reality this side of heaven, but on the other hand, my heavenly Father has my back. There are no random molecules in the universe and no random circumstances in my life.

Therefore, I take what He gives, both good and bad, and I give until He takes. I both embrace the pain and cling to God's sovereignty. To deny the one leads to pretense; to deny the other leads to hopelessness.

Living My Loss Out Loud

Living with the seeming incongruity between God's loving sovereignty and the intensity of personal tragedy is something I understand theologically. In fact, I understood it even before entering my valley of the shadow of death. Yet once there, the implications, so up close and personal, were extremely painful. Following Carol's death, I was open and frank with our congregation about what I was going through. It was the fall of 2006, which proved to be an unusually rich time for our church. We were in the middle of relocating our campus, and suddenly, with the death of the senior pastor's wife, everyone knew there were bigger issues at stake than bricks and mortar—much bigger issues, life-and-death issues.

Not many congregations have watched their senior pastor go through something like this. Acutely aware of that, I had the deep sense that I needed to honor God by trusting Him and yet be open about my pain, my hurts, my grieving process. I didn't realize it at the time—I was just trying to be faithful—but preaching every Sunday, regardless of how I felt, actually began months of healing for me and months of unprecedented spiritual growth for our people.

As I look back, I am amazed that Sunday after Sunday I didn't dissolve into a puddle of tears. Frankly, all the tears I shed during the week enabled me to get through Sundays; I was "cried out." Never have I sensed God's grace, God's strength, and God's presence as I did during those early months. In the act of preaching and in all the hours of preparation, I was forced to think through what I really believed about God and His purposes; I was forced to pray when I didn't feel like praying; and interestingly, because of the public nature of the pulpit, to a large extent I was able to forget about myself and focus on our church.

If you had told me a couple of years before all this happened that I was going to lose my best friend and then my wife, I would have predicted that I would have to be checked into a psych ward afterward. There just would be no way I could make it. But I am stunned by the peace and the contentment God gave me.

That grace enabled me to begin boldly proclaiming some truths to our church body that first fall, even on those Sundays when I had just endured another horrendous week. Now I want to pass them on to you.

I long for you, Christ follower, to be stronger, to be assured of God's sovereignty and care in the midst of pain. That is why I tell this story even as I weep, even as I continue to grow and learn, and yes, struggle.

CHAPTER 1

Into the Depths

IN LATE JULY 2005, Carol, two of our kids, and I were visiting our oldest daughter, Shannon, in Denver. Over the years our family had spent a fair amount of time in Colorado, sometimes skiing in the winter, sometimes hiking in the summer. We loved it, and as a busy pastor, I found the majesty of the mountains a great way to "reset" spiritually. During several summer trips our family even hiked a handful of Colorado's fourteeners, or peaks over 14,000 feet.

That summer day, Carol, Alissa, Ryan, and I were climbing a relatively tame fourteener near Denver, but as always even the "easy" ones were strenuous for us flatlanders from Illinois. To my chagrin, Carol beat me to the top. Always healthy and in great shape, she embarrassed me, so I mumbled something about having to wait for eleven-year-old Ryan when I caught up with her.

The trip was bittersweet for us. Just a few months before, our close friend Tom had died after a grueling battle with cancer. Even as we continued to mourn Tom and talk about him, we were thankful for this break, knowing when we returned home we would be jumping into another busy fall.

I considered Carol my partner in ministry as well as life. Scary smart, she was able to grasp abstract concepts in a millisecond and discuss them perceptively. During my last year of seminary, shortly after we married, we took a senior seminar together. I was the seminary student; Carol merely audited the class. This nontechnical course, made up of fewer than a dozen students, explored the issues of power and authority in the New Testament. Our professor was Duane Litfin, who would later become my boss, my mentor, and our lifelong friend.

While an undergraduate, Carol had read widely on the debate over women's roles in the home and church, and had a surprising grasp of the literature. Almost immediately Duane picked up that this young lady was way ahead of the rest of the class, on both the conceptual and practical levels. Neither I nor my classmates had much to add to their energetic dialogues. About halfway through the course, Duane stunned us, asking Carol and me to help him write a book on this very topic. Actually, he really wanted my wife as a collaborator but figured he had to invite me to participate as well!

Though I sometimes struggled with certain sections of

C. S. Lewis or G. K. Chesterton (don't most of us?), as Carol read these authors she would discuss them with me in a way that showed she had already grasped their significance. Sometimes after I explained my interpretation of a passage, she would say, "No, here's what I think he means. . . ." Time after time I would discover she was right. She was both my biggest fan and my most helpful critic, periodically asking after a sermon—and always with a smile—"Honey, why in the world did you say that!?" Quickly she would suggest what I might have done differently. Only very rarely did I disagree.

So, having just walked through the illness and death of Tom along with his wife, Rhonda, I was grateful as never before to know I had Carol to lean on as Wheaton Bible Church prepared to launch a new ministry year. Boy, did I need her input and support.

My friend, Dr. Tom Williams, was one amazing guy. He was a highly respected general surgeon—so respected that he became the president of the medical staff at Central DuPage Hospital, one of the major hospitals in the western suburbs of Chicago. In his position, he represented about eight hundred doctors, including his wife, who was a pediatrician.

Tom was also a leader in our church, a man's man, a man other men looked up to, because he was different from many of us—not weird, just much more bold. Simply put, Tom loved telling people about Jesus. He was deeply convicted and passionate about Christ and sharing his faith in a way many of us aren't and don't. When Tom spoke, people listened. Tom was always sharing the gospel (trust me, that's not an overstatement) with patients, doctors, neighbors, and friends. But he was so easygoing, so smooth and winsome, that everyone loved him. Tom was unusually upbeat and joyful. I loved his sense of humor; a consummate servant, he was caring, sensitive, and regularly looking for ways to help others.

Some years before, a doctor in our area hit a wall. His marriage was falling apart because of bad choices he had made. To complicate matters, he was sinking fast into a deep depression, becoming almost nonfunctional. Tom lovingly but boldly stepped into the crisis, befriending this physician and leading him to the Lord. Tom insisted this man move from the hotel where he was staying into Tom's home so Tom could disciple him through his ordeal. He lived with the Williamses for months.

When I ran into this doctor years later, he was a changed man. Active in his church out West and practicing medicine once again, he told me that Tom Williams had "saved" him. So many others have said the same thing.

But Tom did more than talk. In addition to leading evangelistic Bible studies, he passionately discipled younger Christians, always inviting them into his life. Tom was no respecter of titles or status, and the Bible studies he led were always attended by a crazy cross section of construction workers, bikers, and men struggling to land on their feet in Christ. As much as anything I knew about Tom, the diverse composition of these groups revealed the unusual breadth of his love and the clarity of his vision about the nature of the body of Christ.

Tom and Rhonda often gave away 50 percent of their income. They drove older cars, hosted and housed missionaries, and regularly reached out to people in crisis.

Tom had a huge heart for evangelism and missionaries. He started an orphanage, medical clinic, and ministry to gypsies (the Roma) in Romania just after the Iron Curtain collapsed. In fact, that mission is still going today (the medical clinic has been renamed The Thomas E. Williams Mission Center). Right before Tom got sick, he was in Cuba teaching doctors, nurses, and medical students how to share their faith in Christ in the face of communism.

When I get to heaven, one of the questions I want to ask God is why He didn't give the church more people with the gift of evangelism, people who love telling others about Jesus. Our churches are full of people with wonderful gifts, and we couldn't function without the gifts of helps (or serving), mercy, encouragement, and more. But the gift of evangelism seems rare. Tom Williams had it in spades. I guess you could also say he was just much more obedient to the great commission than most of us.

Tom was always challenging me, his pastor, to be more evangelistic. During the early stages of our church's relocation project, we were waffling under the enormity of what we were considering doing. It was Tom who repeatedly spoke up and called us to be strong and outward oriented. As much as anyone, he got us over the hump. At one large all-church meeting near the end of his life, Rhonda read a letter written by Tom, who was too sick to attend. In it he admonished us to press forward so we could reach more people for Christ. That letter was a metaphor for his life. Never lapsing into self-pity or self-centeredness, Tom Williams was consumed with honoring Christ by reaching people for Christ, even as his health was failing.

Daredevil Doctor

I don't remember how Tom and I met. But not too long after I came to Wheaton Bible Church in 1994, our families, along with a couple of other families in our church, started taking vacations together. Almost every spring break a large group of us would go snow skiing in Colorado. Tom's parents had a winter home in Silverthorne, so Tom and Rhonda had been going to Colorado for years. Tom was one of the fastest skiers on the mountain, always. He was fearless. My kids, as they got older, loved skiing with him. I was too slow for them, but not Tom.

One day when we were high on a mountain in Colorado, Tom and his brother Jeff took off into a wooded area for tree skiing; none of the rest of us were good enough or brave enough to go along. At the bottom of the mountain when we reconnected, Tom said he had hit a jump with about a fifteen-foot drop. As he was flying through the air, his tips crossed as he headed straight for a tree. If you're a skier, you'll understand the problem. Tom said he thought he was going to meet Jesus right then, but he missed the tree and survived with a major wipeout.

Afterward I asked him if he felt like continuing to ski, and he said, "Sure, I'm just swallowing a bunch of blood, but let's go." Tom was unfazed—swallowing blood, no big deal. I would have gone straight to the clinic. Not Tom. He loved life and was a natural risk taker. Perhaps it was inevitable: he was one of five boys and was born in Syria where his father, also a surgeon, was on a medical missions assignment until the country's political situation forced the family to leave.

I, too, am a risk taker. I used to be a competitive water-skier, a ski jumper. One of my great claims in life is that I got Tom and some other good friends in our church involved in the extreme sport of barefoot waterskiing. I thought of it as my Monday morning discipleship ministry on the river! Tom would tell his medical staff he was unavailable to see patients for a couple of hours and we'd head to the water. We would laugh uncontrollably at our own brutal wipeouts, and even more over the ones taken by the unsuspecting people we were attempting to teach. (Yes, I know that surgeons and pastors should be more mature, but that's a different matter.)

Over the years Tom and I owned three different ski boats together, each time trading an older model for a newer one. People say if you want to wreck a relationship with a friend, buy a boat together. Tom and I, however, never had a single issue—not even on that Father's Day some years ago when he sank our second boat in four feet of water and made me retrieve it the next day . . . something about his being "too backed up with surgeries to help."

We spent long summer days with our families and friends

doing crazy things on the water. Tom and I and some others would go down to Florida to learn new tricks from one of the best barefooters in the world. Then we'd take our kids there to ski—barefoot, of course—sometimes on lakes where we had to keep our eyes open for alligators we had seen earlier.

I got Carol to barefoot once, very briefly. But after doing a face-plant (that's skiers' lingo for a bad, face-first wipeout) at thirty miles an hour, she told me, "Never again." She said a few other things as well! It was a bad scene—one of several times in our marriage when I pushed her too hard.

Tom and I were passionate about the Kingdom and about life, and out of that we forged a great friendship. When Tom came over to our house, he never knocked—he just walked in and announced himself, sometimes startling my wife. One day when her parents were visiting from Texas, Carol's mom yelled out, "There's a guy riding circles around the house on a motorcycle!" Calmly Carol said, "Oh, that's Rob's friend Tom. He must be done with surgery." Friendships like this are both so very precious and, unfortunately, so very rare.

Tom loved his Harley, the University of Iowa (his alma mater), Chicago Bears football, Cubs baseball, coaching his younger daughter's travel softball teams, and strangely, driving semitrucks. That's right. He would drive fully loaded semi-trailer rigs across the country. One time Tom picked me up with my then-four-year-old son and we went driving around Chicago in a semi. Tom's great frustration was that he couldn't get more truck companies to let him drive rigs. They didn't want to pay the hefty insurance to cover a surgeon. Duh!

Our strengths, left unchecked, can become weaknesses, and one of Tom's shortcomings was that his wide variety of interests meant he was often on the move. This frustrated his wife, Rhonda, and created tension between them at times. While it was not an insurmountable problem, it was an issue. Men love their toys and their hobbies, and Tom was no exception. They were a release for him.

However, in the main, my buddy Tom was a great husband to Rhonda and a great father to his three kids, Nathan, Kelly, and Christine. He was always looking for ways to spend time with them. He deeply loved Rhonda and took the spiritual leadership of his family seriously. I know, because Tom and I were accountability partners for a number of years, meeting every other Thursday to check in spiritually and to pray for our kids, our marriages, our church, and lost people. Tom was so committed to Christ that just one month before he was diagnosed with cancer, he told me he felt like we needed to start meeting every week, because there was too much to talk about, too much to pray about. I agreed, but God had other plans.

Rare and Deadly

The cancer first emerged as a lump in Tom's throat. Early on, he was suspicious but thought it was likely a highly treatable thyroid issue. That Christmas the Williams family went to Hawaii, not knowing this would be their last vacation together. The lump kept growing, and on New Year's Day when their family was back and over at our house, Tom was having trouble swallowing and talking. A couple of days later, Tom went to the doctor. Unfortunately, tests and surgery indicated he had a very rare and untreatable cancer—squamous cell carcinoma of the thyroid. The thyroid expert who operated on Tom said it was the first time in 12,000 surgeries that he had seen this.

Just before beginning chemotherapy and radiation treatments, Tom e-mailed an update to family and friends. He wrote:

> I hope you love life and others as God would have you to do. Please keep praying for me and my family. This is tough, tears come easy, and that's ok. I wonder if God has been preparing me for 50 years to handle this.

Even though Tom worked in the midst of a medical community and some of the best medical minds in Chicago were willing to do anything for him, neither chemo nor radiation were able to stop the spread of his cancer. His condition quickly worsened. Soon Tom lost his ability to swallow and therefore to eat and had a feeding tube surgically implanted in his stomach. Soon it became harder and harder for him to talk. When we would sit together in his sunroom that spring, Tom would shake his head and whisper, "I'm okay with this, but isn't this unbelievable?"

Amazingly, I never heard Tom complain. His faith in Christ was a rock for him, and up until the very end of his life Tom was talking about who he could minister to and who he needed to talk to about Jesus, especially other doctors. His biggest concern was for Rhonda and the kids. Like any good husband and father, he hated the thought of being taken from them, as any good husband and father would, even if temporarily.

Our time together, for me, was sacred as we talked openly about what was happening. Tom had no fear, no anger, and more profoundly, he had a deep sense that his Lord would sustain him, even as death was hurtling toward him like an oncoming truck that had lost control on the ice. He continued to radiate perpetual joy, as only someone who was focused on Jesus could.

Tom's final e-mail asked for prayer as he prepared to undergo major surgery. Referred to as a "commando" procedure, the operation was designed to stop the rapid tumor growth in his neck and to alleviate the increasing difficulty he had breathing. This radical surgery involved removing most of the interior of his neck, except vital blood vessels and his windpipe. It even included bringing up part of his stomach and attaching it to the base of his tongue.

In that last message, he said:

Rhonda and the kids are hanging in there and glad that something is going to be done to try to beat this tumor.
I will be out of touch by e-mail for a while.

My life is as always in His hands.

He ended his note with a Scripture that now had special meaning for him.

Indeed, in our hearts we felt the sentence of death. But this happened that we might not rely on ourselves but on God, who raises the dead. He has delivered us from such a deadly peril, and he will deliver us. On him we have set our hope that he will continue to deliver us, as you help us by your prayers. Then many will give thanks on our behalf for the gracious favor granted us in answer to the prayers of many. (2 Corinthians 1:9-11)

Tom died on May 14, 2005, two weeks after that surgery, following a brief five-month battle. He was surrounded by his family with Rhonda lying by his side. She would say afterward that she felt his "first breath" in heaven as he breathed his last on earth.

Tom and Rhonda were just three days away from celebrating their twenty-fifth wedding anniversary. Nathan, their oldest child, was twenty-one; Kelly was eighteen; and Christine was fifteen. I conducted Tom's funeral; the receiving line at the visitation was so long it took the family ten hours to greet everyone. Months later, I spoke at the opening of the beautiful, large, multistory garden area near the center of Central DuPage Hospital, which was dedicated to Tom and named the Tom Williams Memorial Garden.

That summer I sold our boat. A part of me died again that day. I knew life would never be the same without Tom. I had started reading Randy Alcorn's book *Heaven* to help me deal with this loss. The book was hugely meaningful to me, and later I would let Randy know so. I had no idea, though, how much I would need to be fixed on heaven in the days to come. My disappointment had just begun.

An Uncommonly Good Marriage

By the summer of 2005, Carol and I had been married for twenty-six years. We had met in Dallas in 1978, after Carol's sister Karen and her husband, Ken, fixed us up on a blind date. Ken was a fraternity brother of mine in college, and I was instrumental in his coming to Christ. Right after college Karen, Ken, and I did a Bible study together. Karen and Ken repeatedly mentioned Karen's younger sister, who was at the University of Wisconsin. After graduation Carol came to Dallas for an internship. Not long after she had moved in with Karen and Ken, they called me and the four of us went to play tennis. Four and a half months later, Carol and I were engaged.

Carol said she married me because she thought I was funny and she loved to laugh. She enjoyed the comedian Steve Martin, and on New Year's Eve when our girls were little we would always watch Peter Sellers in his Pink Panther movies. Carol would laugh so hard she'd cry.

One summer when we were waterskiing in Arkansas, she and her friend Joan went out shopping and returned to the lake sporting new tattoos. I was shocked; this was so out of character for Carol, a pastor's wife. Only later did they reveal that these were temporary, something intended to help us lighten up a bit!

Our family, especially our kids, and our friends knew what an uncommonly good marriage we had and how happy we were. They also knew so much of it had to do with Carol. I am a type A, pushy, bossy, "take no prisoners captive" guy; Carol, the fourth of five children, was laid back, gracious, easy to be with, constantly upbeat, unusually selfless, and able to keep the main thing the main thing. She didn't have a materialistic bone in her body.

Carol always prioritized people over tasks and was an amazingly gracious, unflappable hostess, always making the many people coming in and out of our home feel welcome. Our daughter Alissa remembers that on a couple of occasions, Carol got so busy attending to others that she forgot to pick Alissa up from soccer practice or school.

More often than not, Carol was several days behind on her to-do list, but if you stopped to talk to her, she was completely focused on you, leaving the impression that she heard every word and that she cared deeply. That's in contrast to me; I often struggled to listen, especially to the kids. I would ask a question without waiting to hear the answer. As Rocky Balboa said, Carol filled in my gaps.

She was an avid reader who loved the works of Amy Carmichael and Elisabeth Elliot, not to mention Agatha Christie, Dorothy Sayers, and C. S. Lewis. We talked concepts a lot. We played tennis, worked out together, climbed mountains, traveled, and skied. A stay-at-home mom, Carol was a phenomenal mother, and our four kids were the beneficiaries. Carol loved Jesus and loved God's Word, having come to Christ in high school through the ministry of Young Life. Then at the University of Wisconsin, where she took part in Bible studies through InterVarsity Christian Fellowship, Carol's faith became her own.

After we moved to Chicago in 1994, we saw God do amazing things in people's lives in our newly constructed subdivision. A number of our neighbors came to Christ and ended up in our church. I am convinced it all began with the women's evangelistic Bible study Carol and another woman started and led for years. Like Tom, Carol cared deeply about people who were living apart from Christ. Some of Carol's favorite experiences were our mission trips into the Amazon jungle or the interior of Ethiopia. Carol loved our church's missionaries and would weep with joy as she listened to their amazing stories when we visited them on the field. Not surprisingly, she was deeply loved inside and outside the church.

Some have said she was one of those rare people whom you knew spent a lot of time in God's presence. My daughters still talk about Carol's tattered sheets of daily prayer requests and her highly organized prayer journal, in which she charted whom and what she would pray for each day. One of the girls' most enduring memories of their mother is coming downstairs in the morning to find Carol sitting at the kitchen table, Bible and prayer sheet spread out in front of her as she sipped hot chocolate.

Perhaps Carol's biggest struggle—not uncommon for stay-at-home moms and even pastors' wives—was an ongoing battle with significance. But let me be careful here.

Carol was a highly intelligent, confident woman, deeply secure in her identity in Christ. However, I was busy with ministry and getting lots of affirmation from it. Carol was a behind-the-scenes servant, trying to keep the house in one piece and our four kids occupied. At times, something deep in her felt that her contribution as a stay-at-home wife and mom wasn't good enough, significant enough, and she would get really discouraged. Carol didn't struggle with personal significance—she knew exactly who she was in Christ and what was important—her battle was that she felt what she did didn't matter that much.

I can still hear her saying, "Rob, people tell you that you are great all the time. Very few people affirm me." It didn't help that I wasn't particularly sympathetic and tended to minimize her pain. I, frankly, didn't get how she could feel this way. But she did, and she had her dark moments. At times, Carol felt passed over because she concluded (wrongly!) that she wasn't that interesting. Some of this was birth order, some of it was normal family-of-origin stuff, and a lot of it stemmed from her stage of life (a stay-at-home mom with young children). By watching this beautiful, competent woman struggle, I learned that when I stand up to preach on Sunday, I'm speaking to all sorts of people who look really good on the outside but who are struggling on the inside.

There's a section in Eugene Peterson's book *A Long Obedience in the Same Direction* that Carol told me both described her feelings and helped her work through them. It's about feeling passed over because we assume God has moved on to someone He finds more interesting. Here's Peterson's statement in context:

> All the water in all the oceans cannot sink a ship unless it gets inside. Nor can all the trouble in the world harm us unless it gets within us. . . . The only serious mistake we can make when illness comes, when anxiety threatens, when conflict disturbs our relationships with others is to conclude that God has gotten bored in looking after us and has shifted his attention to a more exciting Christian, or that God has become disgusted with our meandering obedience and decided to let us fend for ourselves for a while, or that God has gotten too busy fulfilling prophecy in the Middle East to take time now to sort out the complicated mess we have gotten ourselves into. That is the *only* serious mistake we can make.[1]

Sometimes Carol made that mistake. But over time, because of her firm and deep-seated confidence in God's love, we both saw these feelings diminish.

Uninvited Intruder

One month after we returned from our summer Colorado vacation, Carol underwent a routine colonoscopy (a rite of passage for fifty-year-olds, at least in the United States). The test results, though, were anything but routine. In fact, the diagnosis, a malignancy, left us shocked. Carol had recently wondered if something was amiss, but never this—she was way too healthy.

As we headed into our own battle with cancer, it didn't take long for us to see signs that God was in control of the situation. As Carol later wrote in a letter to those who had been praying for us:

The cancer was initially diagnosed on Monday, August 22nd. The night before that, on Sunday night, a woman in our church was awakened in the middle of the night and felt strongly that she needed to pray for me. She could not sleep, and studied her Bible (specifically Psalm 116), and repeatedly prayed for me, not knowing why, and in fact thinking she was to ask me to be a part of a ministry she was involved in. She called the next day, only to have Rob tell her that we were awaiting the results of the biopsy. This is not someone I know well, or that I even see very often, yet she was faithfully praying for me. I am amazed at God's ways—that He would have someone praying for me ahead of time, knowing what we would be facing the next day.

Initially we thought Carol was battling colon cancer; later, however, the Mayo Clinic, which did the biopsy and struggled with the diagnosis for a time, informed us that it was a very rare and aggressive internal melanoma.

Just before we were told how serious Carol's situation was, our middle daughter, Kyle, made a major decision that would also help us navigate the challenges ahead. I will never forget the night in late August when she came into our room and sat on our bed. Her car was packed because she had been planning to leave that night for the drive back to South Carolina, where she was to begin her junior year of college. At the last minute, though, she told us, "I just can't go. God wants me to stay; things are too uncertain."

Though we didn't know it that night, with all the travel and hospitalization that was ahead, we could not have managed without Kyle. She helped keep the house running and took care of Ryan, who was in fifth grade. In fact, she never returned to South Carolina. A few months later though, an anonymous donor offered to pay for Kyle's last two years of college so she could transfer to Wheaton College and live at home. Meanwhile, Shannon, who had just taken her first job in Denver, came home as often as she could and eventually moved back home as well. Our youngest daughter, Alissa, was on the front end of a four-year full academic scholarship in Arizona. Not wanting to jeopardize her standing, she continued her studies there, taking just one semester off and bravely going back to school right after her mother died.

On September 6, just a few days after receiving the updated diagnosis, I wrote a brief letter to our congregation, thanking them for their support and reminding them: "We have received e-mails from all over the world and we have been blown away by the love and the community that is so evident in the body of Christ. . . . As many of you know, the church is moving full speed ahead with our relocation plan and we are very conscious that the enemy wants to do whatever he can to knock us off center. So pray for Carol. Pray that the cause of Christ would be furthered through all of this."

The good news was that, other than the malignancy in her lower bowel, Carol's body was completely clear of cancer. Still, given how rare this form of cancer is, we ended up being referred for treatment to the melanoma team at the renowned MD Anderson Cancer Center in Houston. For months, we traveled from Chicago to Texas every three weeks or so for about ten days at a time. Carol's treatment began with aggressive doses of chemotherapy and radiation, followed by surgery to remove the malignancy in early November.

While doctors were initially pleased by how well her operation went, about a month later Carol discovered small lumps on her neck and back. Further tests revealed that the melanoma had recurred in her upper body.

Early in 2006, Carol wrote again to those who had been praying for her:

> I want to thank all of you once again for your prayers. They have truly gotten us through the last few weeks. The time we spent in Houston was very difficult emotionally for our whole family. After such great news post-surgery, it was hard to go down and find that the cancer had spread, and was growing aggressively. There were many tears and much

discouragement for all of us. But I want to share a story with you about what God did during that time to encourage us.

Rob and I talked a lot about our need for hope, especially toward the end of my chemo, and our stay there in Houston. I needed to grieve, and I had certainly done that, but I felt I couldn't stay stuck there forever. I was praying that God would give me hope. I had written in my journal that I needed courage, hope, and strength; underlining those words. When we got back home the Wednesday before Christmas, I spent the evening going through the mail. I had received two books from people while I was gone. Both were on the subject of hope and both written for people with cancer! In the front cover of one of the books, the woman who gave it to me had written a note to me. She started by saying she was praying for me to have courage, hope, and strength—the exact words I had used when expressing my need. Have you ever wished you would get an e-mail from God? I sort of felt like I had. Psalm 139:4 says: "Before a word is on my tongue you know it completely, O LORD." God knew my need before I ever expressed it, and provided for me.

By mid-January, doctors began biochemotherapy, which is designed to make a patient's own immune system attack the malignant cells. On January 26, our church's sanctuary was filled with people who came specifically to pray that God would heal Carol. For several hours, people prayed collectively and in small groups. The one thousand–plus people who'd gathered also listened as Scripture was read aloud, and they raised their voices together singing praise songs. Carol and I also received e-mails from people all over the country and overseas who prayed and fasted that day.

Carol and I didn't fully understand it, yet we knew deep in the core of our beings that God's people were somehow carrying us through this journey as they prayed. The love and care Carol felt were central to her ability to tangibly sense God's love in this crisis. God's people became His hands, His feet, and most important, His voice to her and, in turn, to our family.

As we continued to press into God and pray, we desperately clung to Him for strength—often just for that day or even that minute. Aggressive treatments led to frequent nausea and other unpleasant side effects. But nothing could stop the spread of her melanoma, not even MD Anderson Cancer Center, where it seemed the doctors worked nonstop. By early summer the cancer was taking over more of her body, which led to increasing pain. Carol had a colostomy, which was difficult for her, and near the end of her life she developed sizable tumors all over her upper body, some the size of baseballs, that would bleed and were so painful that she required around-the-clock doses of significant amounts of morphine. This cancer was brutal, ending up in her brain.

Carol, however, was a pillar of faith, grace, and even joy. Like Tom, I never heard her complain or whine. Not once. One night she collapsed trying to get up the stairs to our bedroom. We rushed into the front hallway to help, and while Carol's frustration was palpable, she never uttered a word. Initially, we thought we might beat her cancer, but during the last four months of her life we knew Carol was fighting a losing battle. We fast-tracked our oldest daughter Shannon's wedding so Carol could participate.

Six weeks after the wedding, on Friday night, August 11, 2006, Carol died in her sleep at home surrounded by her four children and me. We were reading Scripture out loud when she died.

The next several days passed in a blur. Our family greeted people for hours and hours during the visitation. A couple of thousand people attended her funeral service at Edman Chapel on the campus of Wheaton College. Our longtime friend Duane Litfin, who was then president of the college, spoke at the funeral. At the time of Carol's death, our daughter Shannon was twenty-four; Kyle, twenty-two; Alissa, twenty; and Ryan, twelve.

I hated this for all my kids but especially for Ryan, probably because it brought back my own painful memories. I was thirteen when my father died. And now the loss of a parent was happening all over again for my son. The circumstances were totally different though. When he died, my dad was an alcoholic who was divorced from my mom. He had little involvement in my life. In fact, his death came as something of a relief.

On the other hand, Ryan had lost his mom, who was incredibly supportive and loving. After Carol's death, I explained to all my kids that grief was normal, natural, and necessary; that it would come in waves; that everyone handles it differently; and that the next months would be really dark but somehow we would get through it. I was particularly concerned about keeping in close contact with my son because he was so young. I encouraged him to cry when the grief hit and listened for his underlying feelings about God and his loss when he asked questions like, "Dad, why is it that my mom died and none of my friends' moms have?"

Lessons on Living

Five years later, I still find it hard to believe all we went through. (I am a pastor—other people's wives die, not mine. I take care of sick people, but our family doesn't get sick.) How did we get through it? We had to trust God as never before. On the one hand, that sounds so simple. After all, we realized early on that we didn't really have any other choice— we were in way over our heads. On the other hand, trusting in God seems counterintuitive when the news keeps getting worse; when you feel helpless to stop the suffering of the person you love most; and when you can't imagine any good that could possibly come from the loss you're facing. I mean, what good can come from a fifth grader losing his mother?

And yet trust is really all we have. I'm convinced that the difference between Christ followers who seem to transcend their circumstances and those who do not is that the first group focuses on and lives in light of divine realities and the other doesn't. The first group isn't made up of stronger people with a greater tolerance for pain; it's made up of hurt-ing people who choose to look up, honestly pouring out their pain and their petitions to the One whom they know is sov-ereign and loving and faithful.

Those men and women in the second group may start out well spiritually, but as trials, disappointments, and difficulties crop up, they become angry. They may be angry at others, angry at life, angry at God—or angry at all three. Sometimes they are too "spiritual" to admit it, but the truth is, deep down, they are really disappointed and frustrated with God.

In the end, your view of God will determine how well you cope with adversity. And that is really what this book is all about. In the coming chapters, I will share stories about how I have seen God at work, even in our family's darkest moments. I'll also unpack scriptural truths that have become richer and more personal to me over the past several years. By the time you finish this book, my prayer is that you'll have a better understanding of how you can turn adversity into advantage, navigate change and grief, and persevere through the hard times into the "hope and a future" God has prom-ised you (see Jeremiah 29:11).

Overcoming deep disappointment isn't just a change from one set of circumstances to another; it's a journey toward increasing likeness to Jesus, a transition that leads to spiritual transformation. This is one way I have seen that play out in my own life: I am a driver and a doer. I tend to be attracted to Kingdom movers and shakers, to a fault. Though I love being a pastor, before Carol became ill, hospital visitation had always been one of the least favorite parts of my job. That changed for me. Permanently.

I have a long way to go on the compassion continuum, but I am at a very different point now. Just getting Carol through the airport in her wheelchair with all her IV chemo stuff was life-changing. I'll never forget watching her try to smile, even as she winced each time she was bumped in O'Hare Airport's crowded hallways.

Sitting in waiting rooms day after day next to very sick patients, including horribly ill children, gave me a whole different perspective on what life becomes for way too many people. I hate cancer and I hate what it does to people. Now, however, I am aware and care in ways I never imagined before.

Your disappointments will transform you in different ways from the way I've been changed. But you will be changed. The grief that Tom's family and my family feel will never go away completely, but we have experienced an unbelievable amount of God's blessing, strength, and joy.

Disappointment isn't antithetical to the abundant life Jesus both promised and secured for us—it's central.

CHAPTER 2

Truths in the Night

A COUPLE OF MONTHS AFTER CAROL DIED, I stood in our laundry room facing a significant pile of laundry. It had been a long day at work—not the best day—and I had just made dinner. (Actually that is an overstatement. I don't cook, so I had simply reheated a dinner someone had brought to us.) I was tense, and I broke.

I looked at the mound of clothing and towels and thought, *I can't do all this; I don't want to do all this. Where did Carol go? She always did the laundry! Why has this happened? I don't want to cook. I can't run our house and take care of the kids. I don't want to be a single parent. This is impossible!*

Raw fear swept over me as my mind darkened and my

stomach tightened in one big knot. Then God intervened—right there in my laundry room! Immediately the laundry room became a symbol of everything I hated and everything I needed. There was no audible voice, but I distinctly heard God tell me, *Rob, you can do this; I will get you through this.* Immediately I was flooded with a sense of peace that, remarkably, has largely continued to this day. I remember that moment as if it were yesterday.

There's no getting around it: deep pain brings us to the end of ourselves and, more times than not, face-to-face with overwhelming fear. This struck me again not long ago when I spoke at a funeral for a twenty-six-year-old man who had committed suicide. I had conducted services for suicide victims before, but this one was off-the-charts sad because this young man had off-the-charts potential. He had simply lost his way. That afternoon I shared some of the bedrock truths God had been teaching me about disappointment and loss. Truths that helped my laundry room become a sanctuary. Truths that gave me peace in the midst of my nightmare.

Please don't misunderstand: recognizing these realities won't make the agony of death—especially suicide—go away. It won't immediately take away all your anger over a job loss, divorce, or a child who has strayed. Nor will it answer the "why" questions. I do not want to oversell. But I can and will tell you, in much more detail here, what I told those heartbroken family members and friends about working through tragedy. And make no mistake, it is work . . . faith-work . . . that enables a person to grieve without losing heart.

So as I addressed the grieving, hurting people who had gathered at that young man's funeral, I offered what I hoped would be something of a lifeline—four truths that I've learned to cling to: (1) we live in a fallen, sinful world; (2) God is wonderfully and completely sovereign; (3) the believer is not home yet; and (4) whoever believes in Jesus will live with Him in heaven forever.

Truth #1: We Live in a Fallen, Sinful World

Cornelius Plantinga's well-written book on sin is called *Not the Way It's Supposed to Be*.[1] I love that title! Suicide, earthquakes, tornadoes, terrorism, war, poverty, rape, murder, self-centeredness, hate, hypocrisy, abuse, adultery, addictions, and human trafficking—they're all products of living in a fallen, sinful world. This isn't pessimism; it's realism, biblical realism.

At the risk of sounding like a killjoy, let me suggest that too many of us expect too much out of life. Our expectations are unrealistic because our view of sin and its pervasive consequences is minimalistic. As a result, we unintentionally set ourselves up for disappointment whenever difficulty comes. So listen carefully, and I say this gently: there's a sense in which we, as followers of Christ, need to lower our expectations, relative to what this life offers, relative to what this life will be like.

When I entered college, I wanted little to do with the Bible, little to do with Jesus Christ or the church, but that all changed when a fraternity brother challenged me during my sophomore year to start reading the Bible. There's much more to the story of my conversion, but as I began reading, it struck me that the Bible is correct—our biggest problem isn't the economy, it isn't a lack of education, it isn't politics; it is sin—the sinfulness of the human heart. My heart and your heart. That made a world of sense to me, even as a happy-go-lucky but lost college student.

As the Old Testament prophet Jeremiah laments: "The heart is deceitful above all things and beyond cure. Who can understand it?" (Jeremiah 17:9). The ancient Israelites, like so many people today, considered themselves righteous and spiritually together because of their religious acts, but God disagreed. He saw deeper into the darkness of their hearts. Likewise, Jesus later admonishes the Pharisees for their phony superficiality. He tells them that it isn't certain foods that make a person unclean before God, it's the human heart. As He puts it:

> What comes out of a man is what makes him
> "unclean." For from within, out of men's hearts,
> come evil thoughts, sexual immorality, theft,
> murder, adultery, greed, malice, deceit, lewdness,
> envy, slander, arrogance and folly. All these evils
> come from inside and make a man "unclean."
> (Mark 7:20-23)

Don't misunderstand. Neither Jeremiah nor Jesus is saying humans are gross, utterly incapable, or incompetent.

They are saying we are fallen and even the best things we do are marred by sin. In other words, our biggest issue isn't our circumstances, it's our heart. The pride, the hatred, the bigotry, the lust, the self-centeredness that rise up within us and cause us to say and do horrible things are indicative of our sinfulness. We sin because we are sinners.

When Adam, as the representative head of the human race, fell in the Garden of Eden, the whole human race plummeted into sin. Paul looks back on this event and affirms, "Therefore . . . sin entered the world through one man, and death through sin, and in this way death came to all men, because all sinned" (Romans 5:12). Some call this original sin; others, inherited guilt.

As theologian Wayne Grudem puts it,

> All members of the human race were represented
> by Adam in the time of testing in the Garden of
> Eden. As our representative, Adam sinned, and God
> counted us guilty as well as Adam. . . . God counted
> Adam's guilt as belonging to us, and since God is
> the ultimate judge of all things in the universe, and
> since his thoughts are always true, Adam's guilt does
> in fact belong to us. God rightly imputed Adam's
> guilt to us.[2]

By the way, Professor Grudem goes on to help us gain perspective on why God is perfectly just to do this. "If we think it is unfair for us to be represented by Adam, then we should also think it is unfair for us to be represented by Christ and to have his righteousness imputed to us by God."[3] Thankfully, the work of Christ undoes the work of Adam for the believer.

But the Fall resulted not just in inherited guilt but also in an inherited sinful nature. So in Psalm 51, David, after confessing his own adultery with Bathsheba, acknowledges the sinful nature endemic to the human experience: "Behold, I was brought forth in iniquity, and in sin did my mother conceive me" (v. 5, ESV). Because David wrote this psalm in the context of his deep remorse over his specific sins against Bathsheba and her husband, Uriah, it's clear David isn't referring to his mother's sexual activity but to his own sinful nature. Paul, speaking about life before Christ, says similarly that we "were by nature children of wrath, like the rest of mankind" (Ephesians 2:3, ESV). My experience as a parent confirms this sobering biblical principle—my kids didn't need to be taught to disobey, it's inherent in their nature.

Further, the Fall had huge ramifications for creation. In Genesis 3:17-18, God tells Adam and Eve, "Cursed is the ground because of you. . . . It will produce thorns and thistles for you." When describing the Fall's impact on creation, Paul uses phrases like "subjected to frustration," "bondage to decay," and "the whole creation has been groaning" (see Romans 8:18-22). Connecting these verses to Genesis 3, New Testament scholar Douglas Moo says God alone "had the right and the power to condemn all of creation to frustration because of human sin."[4] Not only has the human experience been perverted, corrupted, and marred by sin, but plagues and parasites, drought and disease, pollution and famine are all symptoms and results of our deeper problem of sin.

You may not like it, I may not like it, but the Bible is clear: we live in a sinful, fallen world. And it's not something "out there" or external to us; it's something "in here," internal, resident in the human heart/soul.

My point is this—don't be mad at God, be mad at sin! In other words, change your focus. You and I are not to live in denial—and indignation directed toward evil can even have a redemptive effect—but we need to be careful about who or what we blame. I have chosen, for example, not to hate God, but to hate cancer and death and, of course, sin.

When you feel your anger becoming anger toward God, remember that He is big enough to handle it. But then ask yourself, how is it ever helpful or right for a believer to be angry with God? He is all-knowing, loving, and perfect; we are not. So when you get angry at God—and it will happen; it certainly happened to me—confess your anger, repent of it, and walk in submission.

Hannah, a young woman who served as a leader in our student ministry, expressed this righteous indignation about as beautifully as I've ever heard it. Not long after her seventeen-year-old brother, Ben, took his own life—he was one in a series of students at his high school who did so—she posted these strong words on Facebook:

a couple of things to say. So . . . I will say them.

e with the people who say that Ben was wrong for not

ing until things got better. Trust me . . . I want to punch
my baby brother in the face for what he did.

Suicide is sin. There's no dancing around that. I hope no
one denies that. My brother taking his life? Oh yeah. Wrong.
I know a lot of people are sugarcoating his decision with
the despair that he felt. The despair is real when people are
dealing with it. I went through it. I remember struggling with
suicidal thoughts in college. I remember planning out how
I was going to make the hurting stop. I remember being so
smothered by depression, anxiety, panic . . . the despair
is real.

I also know God doesn't give us more than we can handle.
He says so.

1 Corinthians 10:13 says, "No temptation has seized you
except what is common to man. And God is faithful; he will
not let you be tempted beyond what you can bear. But when
you are tempted, he will also provide a way out so that you
can stand up under it."

I believe him. So that means my brother could have
chosen a different way out. We can do all things in Christ.
The times we choose differently end with results that
are not what God intended for us. It never surprises him
(thank God) . . .

That being said, God is bigger than our failed ability to deal with life. That's why he sent Christ to die for our sins. Christ died for ALL of our sins, past, present, future. Including suicide. All we have to do is accept that grace, and hand our lives over to God, who is so passionately in love with us. That is a much better option than trying to live life on our own.

Amazingly, Hannah wrote these words within forty-eight hours of her brother's death. What I find so striking and so healthy is that she doesn't sugarcoat sin; she faces it. She doesn't blame God, she blames sin.

I once heard a pastor remark, "People say—if God exists, why does this awful stuff happen? My response is, if God doesn't exist, why does it matter?" Denying the existence of God doesn't make disappointment and tragedy any easier. Our fundamental problem is sin, not God.

Truth #2: God Is Wonderfully and Completely Sovereign

After I lost Carol, nights were the worst. I hated going to bed, hated being alone. The questions and fears always intensified at night when I was tired and it was dark and quiet. I thought morning would never come. It's easy to panic in the middle of the night.

Perhaps that is why a second truth was, for me, so significant: God is sovereign, and He invites us to rest, really rest in and cling to His sovereignty. Let's look at a few biblical examples. Joseph, whose story is told in the book of Genesis, spent some of the best years of his life in an Egyptian rat-hole of a prison. And this for crimes he did not commit! I can't imagine his disappointment. But amazingly, neither bitterness nor self-pity seemed to gain a foothold in Joseph's life. Years later he would say to the very brothers who betrayed him, "You intended to harm me, but God intended it for good to accomplish what is now being done, the saving of many lives" (Genesis 50:20).

Wow! Joseph refused to remain stuck in unforgiveness because he was resting and trusting in the sovereignty of God. Joseph saw past his personal tragedy to the living, active, personal God of the universe who both transcended and trumped his circumstances.

During Carol's illness, we were given this same gift. We both had a deep, overwhelming sense—better, a conviction—that God was in control and that His good plan for our lives would not fail, regardless of whether Carol lived or died. We weren't pretending and we certainly weren't plastic; we were simply believing and attempting to live in submission to our loving heavenly Father. This is why Carol was upbeat even when she was in severe pain and why I didn't collapse in bitterness and self-pity, especially during those late nights when I had to rush her to the hospital's emergency room.

Joseph, like all spiritually healthy people, was God-centered, not problem-centered, not disappointment-centered, not man-centered. He was convinced that God had a plan and that God was working that plan.

In other words, Joseph believed his beliefs and doubted

his doubts, instead of doubting his beliefs and believing his beliefs. Believing your beliefs enables you to thrive in adversity; doubting your beliefs, on the other hand, will bury you. And because of his conviction that God was in control, Joseph didn't quit . . . on life or on God.

Then there's Job. Notoriously godly, Job "was blameless and upright; he feared God and shunned evil" (Job 1:1). He was also unusually prosperous and wealthy by ancient Near Eastern standards, owning vast herds and employing a large number of servants. Yet in a take-your-breath-away sequence of events, Job lost all ten of his children, most of his significant wealth, and his good health.

Making an awful situation worse, his wife was hardly supportive, encouraging him to "curse God and die" (Job 2:9), while his friends condemned him instead of consoling him. Mistakenly, they were convinced his enormous suffering had to be his fault. Just one of those circumstances would do a lot of us in, but taken all together it's almost unbearable. Imaginable, yes; bearable, no! (By the way, over a century ago Horatio Spafford, author of the hymn "It Is Well with My Soul," was kicked out of his church in Chicago because the leaders were convinced that his suffering, including the death of his four daughters at sea, was somehow the result of his sin.[5])

Yet in one of the Bible's most poignant pictures of resting in the sovereignty of God, we read,

> At this, Job got up and tore his robe and shaved his head. Then he fell to the ground in worship and

said: "Naked I came from my mother's womb, and naked I will depart. The LORD gave and the LORD has taken away; may the name of the LORD be praised." In all this, Job did not sin by charging God with wrongdoing. (Job 1:20-22)

Job's conviction that God was in complete and total control sustained him when everyone else seemed to have deserted him.

But there's more to Job. Many Old Testament scholars suggest Job was the first Old Testament book written. That means the first inspired, authoritative book of the Bible that God gave us is a book on suffering. Do you think our pain matters to God? Do you think God is aware or cares? Don't you think God wants us to know we are not alone, that others have gone before us? And don't you think God wants us to know how to respond when the bottom falls out?

I also find it instructive that, in the book of Job, God never answers the "why" question for Job. God never tells him why he lost any of his children, his livelihood, or his health. He doesn't unpack Job's tragedy. And God could have . . . easily. Instead, at the end of the book when God reveals Himself to Job, He addresses the "how" question—how He wants Job and all His people to respond to suffering by submitting to His sovereignty (Job 38–41). Please, please, dear friend, learn from the book of Job; don't lean your ladder of frustration against the "why" question. Instead, lean into the "how" question. Focus on how God wants you to respond.

Job, then, may be the first recorded biblical hero, not because of his understanding—he didn't get his questions answered—but because of his willing submission to God, in spite of his questions.

As I was going through my own ordeal, considering Job's response to his personal crises was huge for me. He helped me affirm that God is on His throne, in control, and using both the good and the bad in my life as He sees fit (even when I can't see it). Like Job, I came to rest in the sovereignty of God. The apostle Paul—no stranger to suffering himself—offers this comforting promise from God in Romans 8:28: "And we know that in all things God works for the good of those who love him, who have been called according to his purpose." "All things" means *all* things. I have chosen to believe this.

In her book on suffering, *When God Weeps*, Joni Eareckson Tada, a quadriplegic, helped me better understand what the Bible says about the intersection between God's sovereignty and suffering when she wrote: "God permits what he hates to achieve what he loves."[6] James Means, a seminary professor who also lost his wife to cancer, shows what this looks like when someone is in the throes of suffering.

In the days of my grief, my great turmoil tempts
me to charge God foolishly. The truth, however,
is not that He casts me into a black pit to leave
me to wallow in despair; rather, He superintends all
the events of my life so that His purposes might be

achieved. This superintending grace of God includes events distasteful to me, but essential to His plan.

Therefore, I hold God ultimately responsible for my grief because He is sovereign and has permitted cancer to prove fatal. Rather than responding to this truth with bitterness, I worship Him. By faith I trust Him in my pain and believe He is infinitely good in permitting this to happen to me.[7]

Notice the incredible theological balance Dr. Means maintains: "God [is] ultimately responsible for my grief. . . . I worship Him." Wow! What a brilliant and vivid statement of submission to the sovereign grace of our loving heavenly Father.

Let me be blunt. As I mentioned, I couldn't and can't understand how it was good for my son to lose his mom at the age of twelve, let alone my teenage and young adult daughters. And you'd better believe that we fought hard against the disease as it ravaged Carol's body. Yet we had a growing awareness that perhaps God was up to something other than bringing about healing. Our assignment was to learn to deal with it. To submit.

I found my greatest comfort, in fact, in a third and supreme example of submission to the sovereignty of God in the Bible. While in Gethsemane, the night before He was crucified, Jesus said to His Father, "Take this cup from me. Yet not what I will, but what you will" (Mark 14:36). His prayer became a model for my own as I alternated between hope and despair during Carol's illness: "God take this from us. Please take this cancer from us! Yet not my will, but Your will be done."

I prayed this way, not only because Jesus did so in Gethsemane, but because in the Gospels He promises to answer prayer—in His way and His time, of course: "Ask and it will be given to you; seek and you will find; knock and the door will be opened to you. For everyone who asks receives; he who seeks finds; and to him who knocks, the door will be opened" (Matthew 7:7-8).

Like our Lord in Gethsemane, though, we do not stop after bringing God our request. Instead, we move to submission; that is, we balance our aspirations and our desires with submission to God's assignment. We leave the outcome to God.

Jesus' words are extraordinary. Facing the greatest agony of His earthly life (Jesus was fully human), completely cognizant of what was ahead (He was fully God), Jesus prayed the richest words of submission in all of God's Word, words that I personally repeated hundreds of times in my darkest moments; "Not my will, but Thy will be done."

Please understand: just because Carol and I submitted our future to God doesn't mean we liked what we were living through. We were, however, willing to accept our ordeal as God's assignment to us. Was Carol ever scared? Did she sometimes worry? Yes, but she remained positive, knowing she could give her fears and concerns to her loving heavenly Father, whom she believed was completely in control of her situation. Those of us around her could see this peace reflected in her eyes and in her infectious smile.

Less than a month after discovering the first lumps on her neck—a dreaded sign that the melanoma was spreading to her upper body—Carol wrote this to those people praying for us:

> I take great comfort in 2 Corinthians 4:16-19: "Therefore we do not lose heart. Though outwardly we are wasting away, yet inwardly we are being renewed day by day. For our light and momentary troubles are achieving for us an eternal glory that far outweighs them all. So we fix our eyes not on what is seen, but on what is unseen. For what is seen is temporary, but what is unseen is eternal."
>
> I believe God is able to heal completely, and He is also able to use our troubles for His glory. We can trust Him no matter what the outcome, that He will always love us and always be intimately involved in our lives.

From Carol I learned that contentment isn't a function of your circumstances; it's a function of your convictions. The summer of her death, our son, Ryan, was playing baseball. I have vivid memories of my wife, barely able to walk, coming to a couple of Ryan's games. She was thrilled to be there watching her son and was determined to support him. Actually, she thought it a great blessing to be there, even as she winced in pain.

More vivid still was Carol's demeanor on our oldest daughter Shannon's wedding day, just six weeks before my wife's death. When Carol walked down the aisle as the mother of the bride, she was a fraction of herself physically. Everyone knew it—no one more so than Carol—yet Carol's smile filled the room. Instead of being concerned about how she looked, she was thrilled to still be alive. Her contentment because of her convictions was palpable.

You give God your submission; He gives you His peace. You give Him your confidence; He gives you His joy, His hope. Paul, nearly beside himself with the joy and hope available to us in Christ, longs for this in all of our lives, when he writes, "May the God of hope fill you with all joy and peace as you trust in him, so that you may overflow with hope by the power of the Holy Spirit" (Romans 15:13).

Joseph, Job, and Jesus taught me an invaluable secret: central to resting in the sovereignty of God is submission. In spite of all the bad press, submission—especially submission to God—is our friend, not our enemy. Submission is a beautiful thing, a Jesus thing.

The New Testament word for submission is *hupo-tasso*, a compound word in the Greek, a mix of a preposition and a verb, which literally means to "place oneself under." James used it when he wrote: "Submit yourselves, then, to God. Resist the devil, and he will flee from you" (James 4:7). James is telling us to "place ourselves under" the greater agenda of almighty God (and watch the devil run). Biblical submission, born in faith, is the rock-solid belief that God is always loving, always good, always in complete control. It is coupled with a childlike willingness to place ourselves under the authority of God. Submission, then, is both head and heart. It is not a getaway but a gateway—the gateway to peace, contentment, and joy. It's the only way I have been able to sleep at night, and I am a lousy sleeper. Always have been.

Truth #3: The Believer Is Not Home Yet

Jim Harrell, a member of our church and a good friend, began experiencing pain in his left calf in 2001. Always active, Jim assumed he had suffered a minor athletic injury. After all, he seemed to be in the prime of his life. He and his wife, Linda, had been married for over twenty years and had four children, the oldest of whom was in his early teens. He was respected for his work as a consultant on railroad labor relations, and he was loved by his friends for his big heart and practical jokes.

Gradually, Jim realized that the pain in his lower leg was not going away with rest and physical therapy. After running batteries of tests, his doctor called him on a Saturday morning in early 2003 with a grim diagnosis: Jim had amyotrophic lateral sclerosis, also known as Lou Gehrig's disease. A terminal illness, ALS is a progressive neurodegenerative disease that causes the brain to lose the ability to initiate and control muscle movement.

The illness progresses at different rates among ALS sufferers. Jim lived nearly seven years past his original diagnosis—years beyond normal life expectancy with this disease. Yet its effects on Jim were no less brutal. One day near the end of his life when I was with Jim, I noticed that one of the few parts of his body that he could still move was his right hand.

As physically weak as he became, Jim taught me a significant principle for handling tragedy: we, as followers of Christ, are not home yet. Jim would tell you he didn't get that immediately. For the first year after he learned he had the disease, he really struggled. Then a friend asked him to speak to a church group about living as a Christian in the business world. Near the end of his talk, Jim mentioned how much easier it was to talk about God with non-Christians now that he had a terminal illness. Jim's suffering was drawing him to Christ, making him more like Jesus.

In fact, after his diagnosis, Jim had begun leading neighbors to Christ—lots of them. He also wrote countless e-mails lifting up Christ and accepted dozens more speaking engagements, sharing his story with business groups, high schoolers, and college sports teams. I had him share his story in our church's morning worship services several times from his wheelchair as well. When his disease had progressed to the point that public speaking was nearly impossible, Jim produced a DVD of his story, which he had boldly sent around the world and to such places as the White House.

And what was Jim's primary message? Although he'd been a Christian since college, he admitted that, like so many of us, he had spent most of his adulthood more focused on his life here on earth than on what would come next. His prognosis—a few more years at best to live on this earth—changed everything.

"Suffering is the icy cold splash that wakes us up from the complacency of living this life," he said. "We truly don't see God and his purpose and strength without suffering, because we just become too comfortable."[8]

"All our days are short," he observed. "I'm living life with eternity right here. And I know that what I'm doing matters in eternity."[9]

As his body deteriorated, Jim increasingly longed for heaven; more specifically, he longed to be with Jesus in heaven. Jim and I spent hours talking about our eternal destination. Jim loved talking about heaven. He would cry while praying as he thanked God for the promise of his future in the presence of Jesus. He would weep with joy at the thought of getting a new resurrected body. In an e-mail he sent me shortly after I'd given a message on worship, Jim confessed that for most of his life he had cringed whenever he heard about the nonstop worship in heaven. To him, it had sounded incredibly boring. In his note to me, Jim explained how his perspective had changed:

> My view of heaven is radically different than it was even a few years ago. I now realize that all of our experience in heaven will be worship but with an unimaginable variety of experiences and interactions. . . . I am comforted by the Great Commandment found in Deut. 6 to love God with all

our heart, soul, and might. I realize that we will never be able to attain such a love for God in this present age. Once we are with our Lord and sin has been eradicated from our being, we will be able to truly love and worship our Father in heaven. The other aspect of the verse that encourages me so much is the word "might," which refers to our whole being, including our physical bodies. As I sat in church last Sunday in my wheelchair, using my breathing machine, I was overcome with joy at the thought of worshiping King Jesus with my body again intact. To be able to bow, kneel, lie prostrate, dance, and hug my Lord and Savior gives me incredible hope.

In the latter stages of Jim's sickness, he became friends with the author Randy Alcorn. Randy tells pieces of Jim's story in his book *If God Is Good: Faith in the Midst of Suffering and Evil.* By readily sharing his story, Jim impacted so many of us. Perhaps he put it best:

I've seen more accomplished in the time I've had ALS than in the first fifty years of my life. This illness is a blessing because God is really working on my soul. I'm going into eternity with my soul in a lot better shape than if I hadn't gotten ALS.[10]

As I sat by Jim's bed as he lay dying, I realized that Jim had never lost sight of God's sovereignty or God's love for him, something he would experience fully only in heaven. But the game changer for him was a bitter and beautiful mix of his awareness that he had a terminal illness and absolute confidence that heaven was his ultimate home.

He also learned something many of us miss—that one of the great benefits of suffering is the way it prepares and readies us for heaven. What soap is to the hands, suffering is to the soul. It cleanses us as we prepare to meet the Savior. In a real sense, this was exactly what Jesus was offering the rich young ruler. Luke 18:22 says Jesus told him to "sell everything you have . . . and you will have treasure in heaven." If he had made this sacrifice, the rich man could have been set free from his idols while his soul was cleansed for heaven. There, his treasure would have been complete. Tragically, he refused Jesus' invitation.

We see this connection between suffering and heaven in the life of the believer when Jesus says "if anyone would come after me, he must deny himself and take up his cross and follow me. . . . Whoever loses his life for me will find it. . . . The Son of Man is going to come in his Father's glory . . . and then he will reward each person according to what he has done" (Matthew 16:24-25, 27). When you embrace suffering, you gain glory.

In his book *Don't Waste Your Sorrows*, Paul Billheimer points out that God created us to love Him, yet love by definition must be voluntary. That's why God also created us with the capacity for choice: the choice to love God or not love God, to obey God or not obey God. We are not robots.

Giving us this option, of course, made the Fall and sin possibilities. And God knew that. God knew that sin would require redemption, and redemption would require atonement, and atonement would require suffering—the suffering of Jesus Christ on the cross. Therefore, Billheimer argues, from all eternity suffering has been a part of God's plan.

As staggering as that is, the point I want to make is that suffering is also a part of God's plan *for us*. As Billheimer says,

> All the circumstances of this life are arranged for
> this one purpose: to enable one to learn agape love
> in order to be qualified to administer the law of
> love in eternity. Natural affection does not have to
> be learned, but agape love is learned only by being
> utterly broken, by suffering without resentment.[11]

Heaven is the endgame. Heaven is our final destination. And you couldn't spend too long in the presence of a man like Jim Harrell without realizing that heaven matters now! Heaven changes things. It sifts things. It infuses the Christian with perspective and rekindles hope. It makes us weep for joy. In my three decades of pastoring, never have I met anyone so joyfully focused on heaven as Jim Harrell.

This is all very countercultural and counterintuitive, even for us as Christians. That's why the author of the book of Hebrews encourages us to "fix our eyes on Jesus, the author and perfecter of our faith, who for the joy set before him endured the cross, scorning its shame, and sat down at the right hand of the throne of God" (Hebrews 12:2). This is not complicated. The joy set before Jesus was heaven, specifically His restoration to the immediate presence of God there. In turn, our great privilege and great opportunity is to fix our eyes on the One whose eyes were riveted on heaven. If heaven was central to Jesus' focus in this life and if Jesus is all knowing, can our focus be on anything better? So Hebrews 12:3 adds, "Consider him who endured such opposition from sinful men, so that you will not grow weary and lose heart."

And keep in mind what heaven will be like. Randy Alcorn reminds us in his book *Heaven* that it is a real, physical place created for real people to live forever in the presence of the one and only real God of the universe and His Son, Jesus Christ, with new but very real and physical resurrection bodies. There is a new heaven, a new earth, and a new Jerusalem coming, according to Revelation 21 and 22. The new Jerusalem will have streets, rivers, and fruit trees—all the stuff of a very tangible, physical place. Therefore, the common misperception that heaven will be a boring place (as mentioned by my friend Jim in his e-mail) where we just float on clouds and strum harps is shortsighted and biblically inaccurate. We will have cities, not to mention a universe, to explore; untold and unimaginably privileged service to render; worship to experience; and all sorts of things to learn, people to meet, and loved ones to reunite with.

Alcorn talks about receiving people into our heavenly dwellings.[12] Personally, I can't wait to have dinner with the likes of David and Job; Martin Luther; and Dietrich

Bonhoeffer! And while I love the Google Sky Map app on my smartphone, I know it will pale in comparison to learning new-creation astronomy in heaven; can you imagine the celestial light shows?

This life is not all there is. According to Jesus, death isn't a termination for the believer, it's a transition. Life on earth is a temporary assignment. As Billheimer points out, God uses this life to prepare us for the next one. We are not home yet. Jesus told His followers, "You know the way to the place where I am going." (John 14:4). Do you? Jim, Tom, and Carol did.

Truth #4: Whoever Believes in Jesus Will Live with Him in Heaven Forever

Not too long ago, my small group did a get-to-know-you exercise called "Three Truths and a Lie." You probably have heard of it and maybe even done it. You make a list of statements about yourself; three are true and one is a lie, and you try to fool people about which is the lie. It's quite fun and a good excuse for us pastors to lie, which we don't get to do very often!

I've added a couple of true statements, but here's essentially what I shared with our group about me.

1. I was robbed in an airport in Eastern Europe by a soldier holding a machine gun.
2. I spent a night in jail for a DUI.

3. I chased a bear out of a campsite in the middle of the night.
4. I punched my alcoholic father in the face.
5. I barefoot water-ski on lakes where there are alligators and make my kids do the same.
6. I lived such a wild life that decades later my old friends are astonished that I'm a pastor.

Based on what I told you in chapter 1, you might remember that number 5 is true. The lie here is number 4. My father was an alcoholic, but I never punched him; I never even came close. I just felt sorry for him, actually. I really didn't know him.

What I want you to notice in this exercise is that my life has been totally and radically transformed by Jesus Christ. My life of faith began way back in 1973 in Dallas—in the fraternity house where I was living, no less. When that happened, when God drew me to Himself, everything—I mean everything—changed for me. The purposelessness and emptiness I had felt as I bounced from one party to the next was immediately replaced with a deep love relationship with Christ and an overwhelming sense of significance and mission. Life suddenly made sense. The dots connected.

I want that for you, too. Why? Because according to God's Word, we don't need tips, we need transformation. That is, you and I don't need spiritual tips so we can get a better handle on our own lives; we need spiritual transformation of the one life we can't handle—our own. This is why Paul insists in 2 Corinthians 5:17-18, "If anyone is in Christ, he is a new creation; the old has gone, the new has come! All this is from God, who reconciled us to himself through Christ."

Either we are "a new creation" or we are not. To be in Christ, according to Paul, doesn't mean we have better insights or are nicer people; it means we are radically and completely converted. Salvation, then, isn't something we attain by living a certain way; it's a miracle we receive. As Francis Chan says over and over in his book *Crazy Love*, salvation is to be obsessed with Jesus—and the obsession is a gift of God. New creatures have a new obsession!

Salvation is by faith alone, through grace alone, based on the work of Christ alone. It is not something you earn or deserve; it is a gift you receive. This is why Michael Horton warns in *Christless Christianity* that our ultimate need isn't for divine assistance in the process of moral transformation, it's for a one-sided divine rescue operation in which our responsibility is to believe. Horton writes,

> Our intuition tells us that if we just hear more
> practical preaching (that is, moving exhortations to
> follow Jesus), we will improve. When this becomes
> the main diet, however, we do not find ourselves
> improving. . . . But bring me into the chamber of
> a holy God, where I am completely undone, and
> tell me about what God has done in Christ to save
> me; tell me about the marvelous indicatives of the
> gospel—God's surprising interventions of salvation

on the stage of history despite human rebellion—
and the flickering candle of faith is inflamed, giving
light to others.[13]

That doesn't mean Christ followers never experience difficulty. But as Tim Keller points out in *The Reason for God*,
"If we again ask the question 'Why does God allow evil and
suffering to continue?' and we look at the cross of Jesus, we
still do not know what the answer is. However, we now know
what the answer isn't. It can't be that he doesn't love us. It can't
be that he is indifferent or detached from our condition."[14]

I have found it enormously helpful to keep looking at the
Cross. The fact that Christ was crucified in my place for my
sins means that God loves me so much that He took my sin
and put it on His beloved Son. Really, I have no worries. I
know God loves me because Jesus died for me.

The New Testament tells us that although our sin has
separated us from God, Christ died on the cross, not because
the Jews or the Romans outmaneuvered Him, but to rescue
us from our sin. To prove that the work of Christ was accept-
able to God, God raised Him from the dead. This is the
gospel. And responding to the gospel in faith is how people
like you and me are made right with God and radically transformed. We were once sinful (truth #1); are now submis-
sive (truth #2); but are still alienated, that is "not home yet"
(truth #3); but one day will live with Jesus forever (truth #4).

According to the New Testament, saving faith doesn't
come merely from believing that Jesus existed (James 2:19

tells us even the demons believe God exists); it comes from trusting Jesus to be our Lord and Savior, our sin bearer and cosmic King. All sorts of Americans believe Jesus existed, just as they might believe a chair in their living room exists. But they aren't trusting Him and Him alone to be their Savior. Saving faith, biblical faith, is like sitting in that chair; it's putting the full weight of one's eternal destiny on Jesus. Period. If you have never done so, come to Jesus. For God's sake—for your own sake—sit in the chair. Turn to Jesus. Trust Him for forgiveness.

When you do, your perspective will change forever. J. C. Ryle, who ministered in England about 130 years ago, explained how to keep the main thing the main thing:

> The Lord Jesus is an actual living Person, . . . deal with Him as such. . . . Cease to regard the gospel as a mere collection of dry doctrines. Look at it rather as the revelation of a mighty living Being in whose sight you are daily to live. Cease to regard it as a mere set of abstract propositions and abstruse principles and rules. Look at it as the introduction to a glorious, personal Friend. This is the kind of gospel that the apostles preached.
>
> They did not go about the world telling men of love, and mercy, and pardon, in the abstract. The leading subject of all their sermons was the loving heart of an actual living Christ. . . . Nothing, surely, is so likely to prepare us for that heaven where

Christ's personal presence will be all, and that glory where we shall meet Christ face to face, as to realize communion with Christ, as an actual living Person here on earth.[15]

As I said earlier, I am a hard-charging, constantly-in-motion, easily reactive controller. A type A. Perhaps that's why the experience in my laundry room just after Carol's death affected me so deeply. In those moments I knew I couldn't do what I needed to do. Not anymore, not without Carol. In effect, the laundry room personalized the death of my wife. It was my tipping point, in the worst way. I felt stripped, hung out to dry, powerless, and overwhelmed. Carol had carried me in so many ways; she was the music of my life. And now the music was over.

But God stepped into my despair, assuring me of His presence and power in a very personal way. My panic gave way to peace, my sorrow to joy, my confusion to conviction.

I realize the four truths we've examined in this chapter are basic Christianity—principles we easily assent to when times are good. Yet each one of them took on new meaning for me as I climbed out of the pit of my grief and began to make sense of life in the aftermath of incredible loss. These truths have, in ways I never experienced before, become deep and sustaining friends. Now I know, based on personal experience, that they will not fail. That's why I commend them to you.

CHAPTER 3

Seeing God Above All, Over All, In All . . . Joseph

YOUR VISION OF GOD makes or breaks how you handle adversity. As a pastor, I have seen this principle demonstrated countless times. On the one hand, I have been stunned by how well people who genuinely know God and deeply believe that He is loving, good, present, and perfect react in extremely difficult situations. They trust that somehow, in ways they can't understand, God is in control.

Less than a month after Tom was diagnosed, he and Rhonda sent this update:

This has been a rough week with chemo and radiation daily. Tom has experienced extreme fatigue (like being run over by

one of those trucks he loves to drive!), nausea constantly,
and the inability to swallow at all. . . . We are feeling
overwhelmed and helpless but are being upheld by our
Rock, our all faithful and all loving God!!

Tom and Rhonda didn't sugarcoat the anguish Tom's cancer was causing; however, they chose to remain focused on
what they knew about Christ—that He would lovingly and
tenderly carry them through their ordeal. Weeks later Tom
commented on the notes he'd received from friends all over
the world: "E-mail is an amazing tool God is using. I sit in
wonder and amazement. Who am I but a sinner saved by
grace, to deserve such love and attention. It's all for Jesus;
isn't that amazing?"

Tom and Rhonda's unwavering trust in God enabled
them to give thanks, even as cancer turned their world upside
down. I've seen other believers show similar faith by their tremendous steadiness, sensitivity, and concern for others even
as their own hearts were breaking because of the horrendous
choices a loved one had made. At other times I've seen it in
the calmness, absence of anger, and red, swollen eyes of a
young mother whose child had just been delivered stillborn.
I've also heard it in the confident words of a man who was
unemployed and struggling with a teenager who was giving
him fits. Most vividly, at least for me, are the many times
I've sat with husbands and wives reeling from the sudden
nightmare of marital betrayal. These men and women chose

to fight bitterness and remain committed to God and their marriages, in spite of the devastation and enormous difficulties that lay ahead.

Then there are fellow believers in countries hostile to Christianity. I am so encouraged by stories of God's people standing firm and moving forward in spite of significant opposition and disappointment. As I write, I am on a plane flying over the Atlantic on my way home from a country where fourteen people were killed in riots during my stay. One group of believers I met recently built a beautiful new community center for the purpose of evangelism and discipleship, knowing it could be blown up anytime in the near future. These believers choose, by faith, to fix their eyes on Jesus (see Hebrews 12:2).

Not too long ago I was in a closed-to-the-gospel North African country with a small group from our church. We were deeply impacted by a former Muslim we met who had converted to Christ along with his entire family and his village. The joy on his face, the strength of his faith, and his crystal clear vision of God and God's global plan of redemption were amazing! He told us he will fearlessly preach Christ even if it costs him his life.

More recently I completed a swing through four Eastern European nations, speaking in several of them. In one country, I was blown away by the testimonies of several pastors who remained faithful to Christ under communism. One of them, now a leading pastor in that part of Europe, saw the government file that described in detail how the communists tried to tempt him, seduce him, corrupt him, and even kill him. Even more painful, the file included the names of informers from his own church. Yet his faith then and now is a beautiful thing to behold. My, how God is using him. He pastors one of the largest churches in Europe, and hundreds of believers are being trained in the Bible college and seminary he helped found.

On the other hand, I have been heartbroken over the dark hopelessness, the acute bitterness, and the seemingly insurmountable pain nonbelievers experience when there is a family, health, or financial crisis. The anger in their eyes and the words that pour out of their mouths are not unexpected but are so very tragic. Without God, all these dear hurting people have are their circumstances. When their situations head south, they are like a person capsized in level 5 white-water rapids with nothing to hold on to in the turbulence. One of the reasons divorce is so prevalent in our society is because of our failure to understand that working through adversity and disappointment—and hanging in there in the face of it—is a means to happiness, not the abandonment of it.

Joseph's View of God

Quite simply, disappointment and loss make no sense apart from God. In the introduction, I mentioned that I hoped to leave you with a theology, or put more simply, a better understanding of the nature of God. That brings me to Joseph, whom I mentioned briefly earlier, one of my all-time favorite Bible characters. Joseph overcame early personal tragedy and imprisonment to become one of the most potent political figures of the ancient Near East; in Egypt, he was second in command. At a deeper level, Joseph's story reveals that what we do in the face of adversity has everything to do with our vision of God, our understanding of who God is, our theology. I want to go deeper with Joseph and offer three illustrations from his life that prove this point and that have deeply shaped me.

1. Joseph's vision of the holiness of God. Genesis 39 takes place in about 1900 BC, when Joseph is just in his late teens.[1] Many of us are familiar, maybe overly familiar, with his story. We know about Joseph being betrayed by his brothers and sold into slavery. Maybe we gloss over it too quickly. For years, I did.

But don't let the matter-of-fact nature of this account fool you. This isn't merely a familiar Sunday school story for kids; this is as much an adult story as any in the Bible. That's because this betrayal was an unthinkable act, particularly in an ancient Near Eastern culture where family bonds and allegiances were so much stronger and more central than they are to us today. In that culture, if an outsider killed someone, that person's family was duty bound to avenge the death and murder the killer. So something dramatic had to have happened to compel Joseph's brothers to repudiate every cultural norm and do the unthinkable—sell their brother. What was it?

Their resentment had been slowly building because of the unhealthy favoritism their father, Jacob, showed Joseph. (Imagine the bitterness and anger you would feel growing up in a family where one of your siblings was dramatically favored over you.) Genesis 37 reports that the brothers' antipathy (the word *hated* is used not once but three times in verses 4, 5, and 8), their white-hot anger (according to verse 4, they were so off-the-charts mad they couldn't speak a single "kind word" to him), and their jealousy (see verse 11) eventually became too much and boiled over. In their rage, they sold Joseph into slavery.

Hear me, friend: Joseph had all sorts of reasons to become a hollow, insecure, bitter, raging, chemically addicted, sexually active young man. Yet this is not the Joseph we get to know in the rest of Genesis, and certainly not in Genesis 39:

> Now Joseph had been taken down to Egypt. Potiphar, an Egyptian who was one of Pharaoh's officials, the captain of the guard, bought him from the Ishmaelites who had taken him there.
>
> The LORD was with Joseph and he prospered, and he lived in the house of his Egyptian master. When his master saw that the LORD was with him and that the LORD gave him success in everything he did, Joseph found favor in his eyes and became his attendant. Potiphar put him in charge of his household, and he entrusted to his care everything he owned. From the time he put him in charge of his household and of all that he owned, the LORD blessed the household of the Egyptian because of Joseph. The blessing of the LORD was on everything Potiphar had, both in the house and in the field.

So he left in Joseph's care everything he had; with Joseph in charge, he did not concern himself with anything except the food he ate.

Now Joseph was well-built and handsome, and after a while his master's wife took notice of Joseph and said, "Come to bed with me!"

But he refused. "With me in charge," he told her, "my master does not concern himself with anything in the house; everything he owns he has entrusted to my care. No one is greater in this house than I am. My master has withheld nothing from me except you, because you are his wife. How then could I do such a wicked thing and sin against God?" And though she spoke to Joseph day after day, he refused to go to bed with her or even be with her. (vv. 1-10)

When I speak about this passage to those in our church's men's ministry, I point out that many men and women start out well spiritually. When they run into trials, disappointments, and difficulties, however, they become angry at others, at life, and at God. Sometimes they are too "spiritual" to admit it, but deep down, they are really disappointed and frustrated. From where I sit as a pastor, anger, which starts as deep-seated disappointment, is a huge problem today, even among Christians. And it poisons us. I personally think it's one of the main reasons pornography is such a problem in our churches; men inappropriately use it to medicate their disappointment and anger.

Now don't misunderstand: it's okay for us to be mad at situations, sin, injustice, and evil. After all, the Bible says to be angry without letting it lead to sin (Ephesians 4:26). I know lots of wives who hate pornography and the corruption it brings to men's souls, and I know many men who hate dishonesty in the marketplace, but these strong women and men do not hate God. Being mad at God is a different matter; it's a slippery slope. Sometimes it's hard to pinpoint and sometimes it happens ever so slowly, but when our anger at a situation crosses the line and becomes anger with God, it diminishes us and can lead to all kinds of trouble.

I say all this because if any teenager, any young male, had a "right" to be ticked off at the world, to feel sorry for himself, and to make himself feel better with a little sexual pleasure because he felt abandoned by God, it was Joseph. He had been cut off from his beloved father, sold into slavery, and forced to go to a foreign country.

But look at the first two words that describe Joseph's response to the proposition from Potiphar's wife: "he refused" (Genesis 39:10). Amazing! He refused to succumb to sexual temptation. Remarkable, especially given Joseph's age.

Let me give you a definition: Virtue is the ability to delay gratification. It's the ability to say no, especially when facing sexual temptation, no matter how crummy or sorry for yourself you feel. It's saying, "This isn't right; I will wait for what's right."

But there's a deeper definition that emerges here. At the

end of verse 9, Joseph asks Potiphar's wife an incredibly penetrating question, a rhetorical one that is more statement than question: "How then could I do such a wicked thing and sin against God?" And then we discover how deeply Joseph believed these words when we read: "And though she spoke to Joseph day after day, he refused to go to bed with her or even be with her" (v. 10).

Talk about spiritual victory! Here Joseph displays a second and much more profound definition of virtue. He shows that virtue isn't just the willingness to delay gratification; it's the unwillingness to violate the holiness of God! For Joseph, then, the key to overcoming sexual temptation, or any temptation, isn't just something you do, it's something you believe; it stems from the deep overriding conviction that your God is holy, righteous, transcendent, and pure. It's a vertical thing, not a horizontal thing. Virtue, according to Joseph, is a function of our vision of God. Biblical virtue, character, ethics, and morality are born in our theology and beliefs about God.

Is it all that surprising that today, in a culture that denies the existence of God, sexual failure is rampant? Isn't promiscuity and moral compromise also evident in many churches? Yet here in Genesis 39, in the face of almost overwhelming sexual temptation, Joseph refuses to succumb to any form of sexual sin because he was absolutely convinced of the holiness of God. He lived in light of the fear of God. Joseph illustrates what Peter says in the New Testament:

As obedient children, do not conform to the evil
desires you had when you lived in ignorance. But just
as he who called you is holy, so be holy in all you do;
for it is written: "Be holy, because I am holy."

Since you call on a Father who judges each man's
work impartially, live your lives as strangers here in
reverent fear. (1 Peter 1:14-17)

Our problem with sexual sin, then, isn't merely pornography or lust; it originates from the lost vision of the holiness of God. What you live and do in a crisis is a function of what you believe. When you see God as holy, you will be pure. Your vision of God makes or breaks how you handle disappointment.

2. Joseph's vision of the power of God. Recently Tom Doyle, missionary and author of the book *Breakthrough*,[2] which describes the amazing things God is doing in the larger Middle East, spoke at our church. The next night, after a dinner out, Tom and his wife, JoAnn, came back to our house and we talked in our family room. Tom and JoAnn told us spellbinding stories of the incredible things going on in countries like Iran, Syria, and others.

For instance, at a church in the Middle East, a man with a withered, useless hand approached Tom and asked him to pray for healing. Parenthetically, Tom and I both received our theological training from the same seminary, a non-charismatic school. Tom told us that in his many trips to the

Middle East, such a request hadn't been made very often, so he was unsure how to proceed. But wanting to be faithful, he gathered a team around the man and they prayed as Tom held the man's withered hand. Tom left, returned to the States, and promptly forgot about the man.

A year later when Tom was back in the same church, he noticed a man waving at him. At first he didn't think anything of it, but the man kept waving and flashing—you guessed it—his hand. And then it clicked for Tom: this was the man he had prayed for a year earlier! His hand had been completely and miraculously restored. Apparently the very next day after they had laid hands on him and prayed, his arm got warm and suddenly his hand was normal.

Sadly, many of us are quick to underestimate the power of God, something our brothers and sisters in the majority world understand much better than we evangelicals in the West. Joseph never underestimated God's power either. Let me explain.

In Genesis 41, Pharaoh, the ruler of Egypt, has two dreams, one about two very different sets of cows and one about two very different types of grain. In each, one is healthy, one is sick. All quite interesting as dreams go. We read:

> When two full years had passed, Pharaoh had a
> dream: He was standing by the Nile, when out of the
> river there came up seven cows, sleek and fat, and
> they grazed among the reeds. After them, seven other
> cows, ugly and gaunt, came up out of the Nile and

stood beside those on the riverbank. And the cows that were ugly and gaunt ate up the seven sleek, fat cows. Then Pharaoh woke up.

He fell asleep again and had a second dream: Seven heads of grain, healthy and good, were growing on a single stalk. After them, seven other heads of grain sprouted—thin and scorched by the east wind. The thin heads of grain swallowed up the seven healthy, full heads. Then Pharaoh woke up; it had been a dream. (vv. 1-7)

In the verses immediately after these, Pharaoh is told by a servant that Joseph (now in prison because Potiphar's wife had falsely accused him of adultery) had the supernatural ability to interpret dreams. In fact, this man had once been in prison with Joseph and had seen him accurately interpret two strange dreams.

So Pharaoh sent for Joseph, and he was quickly brought from the dungeon. When he had shaved and changed his clothes, he came before Pharaoh.

Pharaoh said to Joseph, "I had a dream, and no one can interpret it. But I have heard it said of you that when you hear a dream you can interpret it." (vv. 14-15)

Let's be clear: prisons were not pretty places 3,900 years ago. Even today many are downright awful. Yet suddenly,

Joseph, a nobody as far as any Egyptian is concerned, is released from prison and finds himself standing before the most dominant political figure in the ancient Near East.

If I had been Joseph, the one thing I would be thinking is, *This is my chance to get my freedom and my life back. And I want my freedom and my life back, desperately!* So I, for one, would be very careful not to jeopardize my chances. I would be cautious; and one of the subjects I would want to avoid or at least be very careful about, frankly, would be God. After all, Pharaoh and Joseph had two very different views of God. The Egyptians were polytheists; Joseph was a monotheist, and he would flatly deny that any Egyptian "god" was the real God. Joseph knew the differences. But what exactly Pharaoh knew of early Judaism is less clear. Regardless, Joseph doesn't avoid this sensitive and potentially life-threatening subject. He immediately brings God into the conversation, saying: "I cannot do it . . . but God will give Pharaoh the answer he desires" (v. 16).

Joseph uses a Hebrew name of God, *Elohim*. He is saying that his God—the God of the Jews—can interpret Pharaoh's dreams. Now granted, scholars tell us that mentioning another God, Elohim, may not have been an immediate turnoff to Pharaoh. But my point is, for all Joseph knew, it might have been. Why risk it?

If you are serving in tough places or are surrounded by tough people, whether in your family, at the office, or in your neighborhood, you may wonder what you can or can't say about God and whether it will do any good.

Notice Joseph. At enormous personal risk, Joseph, who had apparently failed sensitivity training and never learned to be politically correct, refused (this word keeps popping up when I think about Joseph) to be intimidated and driven by fear. Not only does he speak up about God, Joseph gives God all the credit for interpreting dreams. I know preachers are prone to overstatement, but really, couldn't this be one of the greatest illustrations of evangelistic boldness (in the Old Testament sense) in all the Bible, if not all of history? You decide.

Joseph tells the Egyptian ruler, "God will give Pharaoh the answer he desires." In other words, Joseph speaks up because of his vision of God; specifically, his conviction about the power of God. He is convinced that Elohim has the power to answer prayer, any prayer, any time. Don't miss this. Joseph is staking his life on the power of God! Notice the correlation here between boldness and belief. When we see God as omnipotent, infinitely capable, and able, as Joseph does, we will be bold.

We see this over and over in the Bible. Centuries later, Shadrach, Meshach, and Abednego face imminent death because of their refusal to bow to a statue of the king. Listen to their bold words:

> Shadrach, Meshach and Abednego replied to the king, "O Nebuchadnezzar, we do not need to defend ourselves before you in this matter. If we are thrown into the blazing furnace, the God we serve is able

to save us from it, and he will rescue us from your
hand, O king. But even if he does not, we want
you to know, O king, that we will not serve your
gods or worship the image of gold you have set up."
(Daniel 3:16-18)

Note on the one hand, the three men's absolute confidence in the power of God. "The God we serve is able to save
us . . . and he will rescue us"; yet on the other, their willing
submission to the will of God: "But even if he does not. . . ."
And they make their gracious but defiant statements to one
of the most powerful men on the planet at the time, the great
Babylonian king Nebuchadnezzar, who, at that moment, is
also furious with them.

Flash forward hundreds of years later to the apostles Peter
and John standing before the hostile and agitated Jewish
Sanhedrin, the Jewish priestly high court of the first century.
When the religious leaders order the apostles to stop speaking
in Jesus' name, they bravely respond, "We must obey God
rather than men!" (see Acts 4:19; 5:29). This is the same
Peter who, just a few weeks earlier, had denied Christ. Now,
as a result of his experience with the resurrected Christ, he
is a changed man and is absolutely convinced of the power
of God. As a result, he is bold in the face of adversity, even
with those, like the Sanhedrin, who also have the power over
life and death.

This is exactly the confidence Jesus advocates when He
says, "Do not be afraid of those who kill the body but cannot

kill the soul. Rather, be afraid of the One who can destroy both soul and body in hell" (Matthew 10:28). Here Jesus ties courage to conviction inseparably.

Down through the ages the people who have moved mountains spiritually; changed cultures for the better; survived the valley of the shadow of death; loved and embraced the needy, the overlooked, and the unlovable; toppled injustice; refused to be silent about Christ; and overcome other insurmountable odds are people who have been bold and courageous like Joseph was here in the presence of Pharaoh. And always, of course, the reason and the root ultimately go back to a deep-seated belief in the power of God.

Her unwavering belief in God's power enabled Carol to face her greatest trial with great dignity as well. Yet she would never have attributed the source of that strength to herself. She knew it came from her passion for God and His Word. The chairman of our elder board gave a telling illustration of this at Carol's memorial service. He said:

> In an early meeting with Rob and Carol, the chairman of our elders needed to borrow Carol's Bible to read a passage from Acts. Now one might ask why this elder needed to borrow a Bible, but we'll let [him] explain that to you. Anyway, when [he] borrowed Carol's Bible, what he found was a Bible that was marked through and through. And not just marked. It was worn out. Carol loved God and His Word. Carol trusted God in her finest

hour and in her darkest hour. Carol did not seek
"the good life." She lived the best life. A life lived
knowing Jesus loved her and provided forgiveness
and eternal life.

The point is not that you will never have any fear; it's that,
like Joseph, you can transcend your fear. As the angel said to
Mary, "Nothing is impossible with God" (Luke 1:37). What
you believe about God makes or breaks how you handle
difficulty.

By the way, when we really believe in the power of God as
Carol did or as Joseph did, we are compelled to take action
and confront the deep issues of the world around us. Sadly,
this doesn't come naturally to most Western Christians.
I am struck by the indictment leveled by Gary Haugen, the
head of the International Justice Mission, in his book *Just
Courage.*

We have been isolated so long in our suburban
Christian cul-de-sac that we tend to imagine most
people live like us. . . . Indeed, many Western
Christians simply have no idea what an utter,
desperate disaster is taking place twenty-four hours
a day around our world. They have no vivid picture
of what life is like for hundreds of millions of people
in our world who live in crushing, spiritual darkness,
humiliation and despair. They just don't realize that
there are millions of people crying out every day

to be rescued from aching, urgent hunger; from degrading and hopeless poverty; from the ravages of painful disease; from torture, slavery, rape and abuse. The vast abundance and isolation on the Disneyland island of the world's affluent communities means that many Western Christians miss God's great calling to a life of heroic rescue simply because they are largely oblivious to the need. They just can't imagine that there could really be any great heroic struggle that would need their help.[3]

There is! Think what a difference the church of Jesus Christ could make in these areas if we really boldly believed in the power of God. May God open our eyes to see both the need and His power.

3. Joseph's vision of the sovereignty of God. In Genesis 45 we see a third aspect of Joseph's vision of God. Joseph is now the number two man in all of Egypt. And don't miss that he is a layman, not a prophet or a priest. He is a busy, highly scheduled statesman. His days are long; his nights, short. He has enormous responsibility and authority. But boy, does he know God! After all the turmoil earlier in his life, now in his middle years he experiences incredible blessing and bounty. Yet he remains unwavering in his faith. (Joseph, like Daniel many years later, is one of the few major Old Testament characters of whom nothing negative is said.)

Now he is face-to-face for the first time in many years with the very brothers who betrayed him. His emotions are raging. We read:

> Then Joseph could no longer control himself before all his attendants, and he cried out, "Have everyone leave my presence!" So there was no one with Joseph when he made himself known to his brothers. And he wept so loudly that the Egyptians heard him, and Pharaoh's household heard about it.
>
> Joseph said to his brothers, "I am Joseph! Is my father still living?" But his brothers were not able to answer him, because they were terrified at his presence.
>
> Then Joseph said to his brothers, "Come close to me." When they had done so, he said, "I am your brother Joseph, the one you sold into Egypt! And now, do not be distressed and do not be angry with yourselves for selling me here, because it was to save lives that God sent me ahead of you. . . .
>
> "Now hurry back to my father and say to him, 'This is what your son Joseph says: God has made me lord of all Egypt. Come down to me; don't delay. You shall live in the region of Goshen and be near me—you, your children and grandchildren, your flocks and herds, and all you have. I will provide for you there, because five years of famine are still

to come. Otherwise you and your household and
all who belong to you will become destitute.'"
(Genesis 45:1-5, 9-11)

What a beautiful picture of absolute forgiveness. Philip
Yancey points out that Joseph's wailing early in this passage
is the sound of a strong man forgiving. It's the sound of
the agony and the deep, deep painful work of extending
forgiveness.[4]

How can Joseph do this? How can he forgive his brothers?
I think the answer lies in his mature and settled conviction
that God has been sovereign in the events of his life, telling his
brothers, "It was not you who sent me here, but God" (v. 8).

At the end of Genesis, Joseph restates this conviction
when speaking to his brothers, who fear that Joseph may
take revenge now that their father has died:

> But Joseph said to them, "Don't be afraid. Am I in
> the place of God? You intended to harm me, but
> God intended it for good to accomplish what is now
> being done, the saving of many lives." (50:19-20)

Joseph believed in the holiness of God (Genesis 39), the
power of God (Genesis 41), and the sovereignty of God
(Genesis 45 and 50). He believed God was in control of
both his good times and his bad times; that God was always
working out His plan; and that He worked all things, good
and evil, together for good. That theological conviction, that

confidence in the rule and reign of almighty God, enabled Joseph to see above the turbulent waters of his life; to overcome the anger, resentment, and bitterness always lurking in the recesses of his fallen heart; and to completely, totally, and finally forgive his brothers. This conviction of God's rule produced a contentment and a graciousness in Joseph that are countercultural in any age.

Even today such settled assurance is a stirring sight. Several years back, Tony Snow was President George W. Bush's press secretary. Before he died of colon cancer, Snow said this in an article in *Christianity Today*:

> I don't know why I have cancer and I don't much care. It is what it is. . . . Yet even while staring into a mirror darkly, great and stunning truths begin to take shape. . . . We are fallen. . . . Our bodies give out. . . . God offers the possibility of salvation and grace. We don't know how the narrative of our lives will end, but we get to choose how to use the interval between now and the moment we meet our Creator face-to-face.[5]

Tony Snow, like Joseph before him, illustrates this key biblical concept: your vision of God makes or breaks how you handle disappointment and adversity. When you see God as holy, you will be pure; when you see God as omnipotent, you will be bold; and when you see God as sovereign, you will be content, gracious, and unusually forgiving.

Our problem is not God; it's our loss of a vision of God. As a result, we are anemic and weak, and often too many of us are just going through the motions. I have learned in my suffering that I am at my best when I am living vertically, in close connection to God. There and only there do I find the power to handle what life throws at me horizontally.

CHAPTER 4

Turning Adversity into Advantage . . . Abraham

PERHAPS BECAUSE I TEND to be a risk taker and want you to be a risk taker for Jesus, I am drawn to the accounts of people who've overcome significant challenges to accomplish great feats. Erik Weihenmayer is one such person.

The summer before his freshman year of high school, Erik was living a nightmare. He had been born with a genetic eye disease and was now gradually going blind, completely and totally blind—one painful day at a time. No longer able to see well enough to walk around by himself, he had to grab on to one of his brothers whenever he needed to get somewhere. He says he reached out for their shirtsleeves "with the terror of a small child being left behind in a department store."[1]

Overwhelmed at what was happening to him, Erik felt life was just about over.

One night that difficult summer, Erik tuned in to a television show that was profiling Terry Fox. Terry had lost a leg to cancer, but instead of lapsing into bitterness and self-pity, Terry ran across Canada, from east to west, on his artificial leg! Using the little sight he had left, Erik pressed his nose up against the TV and watched Terry run. As he did, tears streamed down Erik's face. Something inside him came alive, transforming his sagging spirit and infusing him with courage. Today, a few decades later, Erik is one of the world's leading blind athletes and the only blind person in history to summit the seven highest mountains in the world, including Mount Everest.

Blindness is horrible; it's not the way it's supposed to be. But rather than being defeated by his adversity, Erik is now doing things he never would have done with sight.

Erik had known for years that he would lose his sight, but Karl Wiersum, a lieutenant colonel and chaplain in the United States Air Force, received no advance warning of his own adversity. One day in August 2002, Karl was biking down a road in New Mexico when he was involved in a freak accident. After hitting a storm drain, Karl flipped over and off his bike. He ended up permanently paralyzed from the chest down. As he adjusted to his disabilities, Karl felt as if God had disappeared, checked out—not at all an uncommon reaction when someone experiences sustained trauma. He felt like God had moved on to someone more interesting. But somehow Karl kept believing, kept praying.

And eventually, though confined to a wheelchair, Karl resumed his work as a chaplain, this time ministering to ill and disabled people living in a long-term care center. He also relished his participation in the National Veterans Wheelchair Games.

Because the disabled people with whom he worked could see Karl's own limitations, he was especially suited to help them deal with theirs. Along the way, by God's grace, he turned his pain into something positive.

As you encounter struggles, the same can be true in your life. And by the way, that isn't just self-help talk; allowing God to leverage your losses for His purposes and glory is God's will for you, too. Just listen to the apostle Paul:

Praise be to the God and Father of our Lord Jesus Christ, the Father of compassion and the God of all comfort, who comforts us in all our troubles, so that we can comfort those in any trouble with the comfort we ourselves have received from God. For just as the sufferings of Christ flow over into our lives, so also through Christ our comfort overflows. If we are distressed, it is for your comfort and salvation; if we are comforted, it is for your comfort, which produces in you patient endurance of the same sufferings we suffer. And our hope for you is firm, because we know that just as you share in our sufferings, so also you share in our comfort.

We do not want you to be uninformed, brothers,

about the hardships we suffered in the province
of Asia. We were under great pressure, far beyond
our ability to endure, so that we despaired even of
life. Indeed, in our hearts we felt the sentence of
death. But this happened that we might not rely
on ourselves but on God, who raises the dead.
(2 Corinthians 1:3-9)

Notice the apostle's words here. According to verses 3-7
(the first paragraph in the preceding passage), one advantage
of adversity in our lives is that it enables us to encourage others
in theirs. We help other struggling people realize that they are
not alone, that trouble is part of God's plan for all of us.

Even more importantly, according to verses 8-9, adversity
teaches us to trust God and rely on His power. Why? First,
when we're honest, we realize we don't have any choice because
we are in way over our heads, just as Paul was. Second, when
we're patient, we sometimes get glimpses of the way God is
working His global purposes for us, in us, and through us.
Along the rocky way, we learn that life isn't ultimately about
us; it's about God's global plan of redemption. Adversity,
then, is a friend, not an enemy, because in the good hands of
God it brings us closer to others and to God. We give God
our lives and He gives us the opportunity to impact others
for eternity, to comfort them as we experience His comfort.

In America, where we're taught that happiness and fulfillment come from advancing ourselves, embracing this outlook can seem counterintuitive, even strange. Yet as David

Platt warns in *Radical*, we should not separate the grace of God from the purposes of God. That is, God has not given us His grace that we might spend it on our comforts but that we might use it for His purposes, to further His Kingdom. As Platt says:

> We must guard against misunderstanding here. The Bible is not saying that God does not love us deeply. On the contrary, we have seen in Scripture a God of unusual, surprising, intimate passion for his people. But that passion does not ultimately center on his people. It centers on his greatness, his goodness, and his glory being made known globally among all peoples. And to disconnect God's blessing from God's global purpose is to spiral downward into an unbiblical, self-saturated Christianity that misses the point of God's grace.[2]

Did you catch that? God is somehow using your suffering for His global purposes. Though Erik and Karl are modern-day inspirations to me, I look back much further for proof positive of this truth.

By Faith

You probably know the story of Abraham, the father of the nation of Israel. You can read his account in Genesis, beginning in chapter 12, but I find it particularly illuminating to view his life through the lens of Hebrews 11, which has been called the "Faith Hall of Fame." That is not because the Old Testament believers profiled there were superheroes. Instead they were ordinary men and women like you and me who trusted God—especially in the face of significant difficulty and perplexing questions. Hebrews 11:8-19 centers on Abraham's response to four key challenges. Each time, Abraham met the new challenge by faith (see verses 8, 9, 11, and 17: "by faith" is the section marker or hinge).

When properly understood and applied, these four precepts will help you turn adversity into advantage. Adversity, it turns out, isn't just one of the most common experiences in life; it's one of life's most potent forces with the potential to result in unimaginable good.

Let's look at them one at a time.

1. By faith, obey God, even when He doesn't answer your questions. Hebrews 11:8 centers on the first episode in Abraham's life:

> By faith Abraham, when called to go to a place
> he would later receive as his inheritance, obeyed
> and went, even though he did not know where he
> was going.

This is one of the earliest and most important events in the Old Testament: God's dramatic call of Abraham. Let's go back to roughly 2000 BC, when Abraham was seventy-five years old (and still known by his given name, Abram). Note what we learn about this call in Genesis 12:1-7:

> The LORD had said to Abram, "Leave your country, your people and your father's household and go to the land I will show you. I will make you into a great nation and I will bless you; I will make your name great, and you will be a blessing. I will bless those who bless you, and whoever curses you I will curse; and all peoples on earth will be blessed through you."
>
> So Abram left, as the LORD had told him; and Lot went with him. Abram was seventy-five years old when he set out from Haran. He took his wife Sarai, his nephew Lot, all the possessions they had accumulated and the people they had acquired in Haran, and they set out for the land of Canaan, and they arrived there.
>
> Abram traveled through the land as far as the site of the great tree of Moreh at Shechem. At that time the Canaanites were in the land. The LORD appeared to Abram and said, "To your offspring I will give this land." So he built an altar there to the LORD, who had appeared to him."

Hebrews 11:8, functioning as a divine New Testament commentary on this Old Testament passage, reveals something telling. When Abraham first set out from Haran for the land of Canaan, he did not know where he was going. In other words he had questions.

Do you have questions? I know I do. And while I personally disdain simplistic answers to complex questions ("It's okay; Carol is in glory"), here God seems to provide no answers at all! He comes to Abraham and says, in effect, "Abraham, I love you and have a wonderful plan for your life, but you have to leave everything you know, everything that is familiar and comfortable—everything . . . your foursome . . . your bowling league." Seriously, think about the cost here for Abraham, who lived in an age when family ties were huge and people were far less mobile. God was directing him to do something difficult—without answering many (maybe even *any*) of Abraham's questions.

Counterintuitive, isn't it? Wouldn't it be much more comfortable making major life changes if all our questions could be answered up front? So the first thing Abraham teaches us is that life isn't merely seeking and getting answers to our questions; life is obeying God in the face of daunting, unanswered questions. Man, was this important for me when I saw the pain in the eyes of my kids.

As I mentioned earlier, I have counseled a number of people who are out of work lately, including a few who are losing their homes. They have questions, lots of them, and they are hardly insignificant ones. *Should I move my family to a state with a lower unemployment rate? Should I sell my car to make another mortgage payment, or will I soon need that car to get to a new job? How do I explain to my kids why the family has to move in with Grandma and why they have to start a new school in the middle of a semester?*

I've learned that physical suffering can also unleash questions. And my family is hardly unique. Not long ago I was in Eastern Europe, visiting a poverty-stricken village in Romania with a couple of Romanian church leaders and American doctors. This village is home to many Roma (gypsies), whom most Europeans consider to be lazy, liars, and thieves. Certainly, those living in Roma villages must contend with high unemployment as well as a low literacy rate and low standard of living.

As we were walking through the village, a twentysomething girl came around a corner . . . crawling in the dirt with sandals on her feet and on her hands. She has never walked because her knees only rotate and bend backwards. It was such a stunning and unexpected sight that I wept. Do you think she has questions? As her family peppered our medical team with questions, the doctors realized there was probably little we could do about her condition right now.

When Abraham went to the land of Canaan, not knowing where he was going, he was modeling something for all of us who are tangled up in the deep weeds of life: questions do not trump faith; faith trumps questions. The character of our heavenly Father—His power, His presence, His love— overrules our circumstances 100 percent of the time. God invited Abraham to rest in His character. Specifically, what in God's character can we cling to today? Just two chapters after the Faith Hall of Fame, Hebrews 13:5 gives us the answer, quoting from Deuteronomy 31:6: "Never will I leave you; never will I forsake you." God promises never to leave us; He does not promise to answer all our questions. Cling to His faithfulness.

When we acknowledged that God was not going to answer all our questions during Carol's sickness and death, there were a couple of implications. First, I understood that my prayers for healing needed to be balanced by prayers of acceptance. I had desires, preferences, and an incredibly strong marital bond I did not want cut. As Carol's life ebbed away, I had to submit to God's infinite wisdom, in spite of questions like, "Lord, You are certainly capable of eradicating this cancer. Why won't You do it?" Or the emotionally harder question, "God, You healed so-and-so. Carol is really being used by You, so why did You heal him and not her?" Then there was the question: "What about the kids? How will I ever take care of them like Carol did?"

So even as I prayed like crazy for healing, God gave me the grace to also pray for acceptance. As the cancer spread, her treatment seemed less effective and our prayers for healing didn't seem to be answered, so gradually and reluctantly, I prayed for acceptance.

Philip Yancey helped me with this through a story in his book *Prayer*:

The Bible puts forward two different kinds of faith. The one kind—bold, childlike faith—impressed Jesus, and several times such faith from the most

unlikely sources "astonished" him. Another kind,
I term *fidelity*, a hang-on-by-the-fingernails faith
against all odds, no matter the cost. Abraham,
Joseph, Job, and others of God's favorites in the Old
Testament demonstrated this faith, and the tribute in
Hebrews 11 honors them.

Scientific studies have amply proved the value of
positive, hopeful faith on overall health. A belief in
healing, in transcendent power, has a salutary effect
on the body's actual cells. Millions can testify to
that effect.

For others, however, there comes a time when
it seems clear that no amount of faith will gain the
desired healing. "I have lived with Crohn's disease
for twenty-three years," writes Stephen Schmidt.
"I know the disappointment, the rage, the ongoing
reality that I will not get better. Period. . . ."

I can pray my heart out and shout my
defiance into eternity, but I will not be healed
of Crohn's disease, at least not now, until
some new medical insight or drug is found.
I have stopped asking God for a miracle.
That has not happened for me in twenty-
three years, and for whatever length of time
I still have to be and live, it is not helpful,
reasonable or faithful to ask of God that
which is not possible. That would be magic.

> I am too old for magic, too experienced for
> sentimentality, and too angry and frustrated to
> waste time on a specific kind of prayer which
> in my life would be a prayerful placebo,
> practicing the piety of prayerful impossibility.

Schmidt goes on to say that he has accepted suffering as part of being human. He had to be healed of the need to be healed. Now he prays for strength to endure, for meaning in his suffering, for faith to believe in a good and loving God even when he has to go in once again for a painful surgical procedure. Each day he must live out fidelity faith.[3]

Some might say Schmidt's prayer life illustrates unbelief; I say it models the obedient faith of Abraham. It shows what it looks like to believe and respond to God in spite of our questions. Stephen Schmidt learned to be healed of his need to be healed and instead learned (and none of this is automatic) to pray for the strength to endure, for the faith to take God at His word in spite of his pain.

One of my seminary professors said something I will never forget. He warned: "Don't get stuck on the back side of a question mark." Abraham didn't and I won't. When my dreams of doing ministry with my wife, enjoying grandkids with her, and spending my final years with her were dying, I went through this transition . . . slowly. I refused to fall into the quicksand of unanswerable questions. I didn't weep any less, but I did pray more intelligently, and frankly, this saved me.

The second thing I learned from Abraham's response to God's call is this: ultimately, contentment and joy are found in submission. As I have pointed out, we must submit to the sovereignty of God. Submission also means we are to stand firm in spite of our questions.

Now don't misunderstand. I am not advising you not to ask questions. We did a great deal of research on melanoma and talked to all sorts of medical experts, including the chairman of the department of melanoma at MD Anderson, who personally handled Carol's case. My wife's sister, Kyle, a doctor, relentlessly pursued possible treatment protocols as well. I called the National Institutes of Health about clinical trials, took Carol to four different hospitals, and listened to a few people who told us about alternative approaches. One well-meaning woman even suggested—at a time when Carol was so sick she could barely move, let alone travel—that we should go to Ethiopia for an experimental treatment she had heard positive things about.

While it's natural to continue seeking solutions to our challenges, it's unrealistic to expect that all our challenges will resolve the way we want them to. Theologian Terry Muck has said the difference between city dwellers and farmers is that city dwellers expect every year to be better than the previous year. If they don't get a raise, buy something new, or end up better off, they think they are failures. Farmers don't see it that way. They know there will be good years and bad years;

they know they can't control the weather or prevent a bad crop. So they learn to work hard and accept what comes.[4]

Of course, there is nothing wrong with setting goals. I am a goal-oriented, accomplishment-driven guy. Our church has a staff of one hundred–plus people; goals, which we set by faith, drive most of what we do. But here's the thing: when my wife died, a large part of me became a farmer. I now understand, in ways I never did before, that there are good years and just plain awful years and that I am on a journey with God in this life to places only He understands. Yet when I submit to the call of God, as well as to the changes He brings along the way, I find joy and contentment that make the journey bearable, despite stinging and lingering unanswered questions.

Like Abraham, obey God in spite of your questions. Don't deny them, but hold them loosely. Very loosely. And never let them keep you from God.

2. By faith, wait for God, even when it appears He's forgotten you. God's purposes in directing Abraham to settle in Canaan didn't suddenly make sense when he got there. Hebrews 11:9-10 says:

> By faith he made his home in the promised land like a stranger in a foreign country; he lived in tents, as did Isaac and Jacob, who were heirs with him of the same promise. For he was looking forward to the city with foundations, whose architect and builder is God.

The adversity Abraham faced here was subtle. Yes, he was now in the Promised Land (by the way, this is the only place in the Bible where the phrase *Promised Land* is used). But this passage reveals the cruel irony: Though God had promised the land to Abraham, verse 9 tells us it wasn't possessed by Abraham—he lived there "like a stranger"; that is, he "lived in tents." As a matter of fact, the land wouldn't be possessed by the Jews for hundreds of years. So Abraham was a foreigner in his own land, never possessing what was promised. To add insult to injury, neither his son Isaac nor his grandson Jacob ever took control of the land. On the one hand, he had heard the voice of God, but on the other, the adversity here was unfulfilled dreams, delay, and unmet expectations. Again, Abraham might have asked, "God, if You promised this, why the delay? Why won't You deliver on Your promise now?" or "God, where are You?"

How was Abraham able to wait? Verse 10 answers that question. He was able to remain patient because his hope wasn't in this life. Instead, "he was looking forward to the city with foundations." This is a reference to heaven, to the heavenly Jerusalem. All this becomes clearer when the writer of Hebrews reflects not only on Abraham but on the lives of Abel, Enoch, and Noah (whom he profiles in the first seven verses of the chapter):

All these people were still living by faith when they died. They did not receive the things promised; they only saw them and welcomed them from a distance. And they admitted that they were aliens and strangers on earth. People who say such things show that they are looking for a country of their own. If they had been thinking of the country they had left, they would have had opportunity to return. Instead, they were longing for a better country—a heavenly one. Therefore God is not ashamed to be called their God, for he has prepared a city for them. (Hebrews 11:13-16)

These people were patient because they knew they weren't home yet. Today, we mistakenly tend to think we are in the land of the living headed for the land of the dying. We assume that if we don't get it all, do it all, and experience it all *now*, we'll never get it. Nothing could be further from the truth. We aren't in the land of the living headed for the land of the dying; we're in the land of the dying headed for the land of the living! Heaven is our home. Abraham and his predecessors saw that and lived in light of that. As a result, over time Abraham learned to handle adversity with patience in the midst of disappointment and delay, even though that meant living as an immigrant with unfulfilled promises.

The reality, of course, is that it is easy to get depressed during difficulty, especially when it goes on and on and we are unsettled indefinitely. Years ago British pastor Martyn Lloyd-Jones wrote that a central cause of spiritual depression is listening to yourself rather than talking to yourself. The cure? Turn it around: talk to yourself instead of listening to yourself.[5]

Over the last couple of years when I have been tempted to

give in to self-pity and utter discouragement, I have realized that I am listening to myself instead of talking to myself. One of the main reasons I have avoided depression is because, though I may get to the edge, I have consistently seized God's Word so I can talk to myself about what God says rather than listen to my fluctuating feelings. That resets me, renews me, and gives me patience and steadfastness.

I was struck by the way my friend Tom, in one of his e-mails, modeled this:

> I am reminded in God's Word that all this is temporary. Suffering is a big part of the Christian life that God uses to show Himself and make us like His Son. Jesus suffered for us more than we can imagine and was brutally murdered at age thirty-three so that we can have life and share that life and love with others. I was reading Matthew yesterday and am always amazed at Jesus' life and lessons. I trust you are finding time to read God's Word.

We even see the psalmists reminding themselves to focus on God, not their troubles. For example, twice in Psalm 42 the writer says to himself: "Why are you downcast, O my soul? Why so disturbed within me?" (vv. 5, 11). I love this! Instead of listening to himself, the psalmist talks to himself! In effect, he grabs his soul by the throat and says, *Enough!*

Like so many others, I find the ancient truths of the Psalms to be especially helpful in combating discouragement, even the dark ones like Psalm 88 that acknowledge so poignantly that horrible things do happen to God's people. When we wait for God, He will ultimately come through as He sees fit—if not in this life, certainly in the life to come. He has not forgotten! Heaven is coming. We believe it because God said it. And patience in the midst of terrible disappointment is how we watch our loving heavenly Father turn adversity into Kingdom advantage. Like Abraham, we are all immigrants of sorts, some just more obviously and painfully so!

I'm not a poetry guy, but I like this poem by Martin Luther. I memorized it years ago. Luther expresses in poetry the same thing Lloyd-Jones says in prose.

GOD'S UNCHANGING WORD

For feelings come and feelings go,
    And feelings are deceiving;
My warrant is the Word of God,
    Naught else is worth believing.

Though all my heart should feel condemned,
    For want of some sweet token,
There is One greater than my heart
    Whose Word cannot be broken.

I'll trust in His unchanging Word,
    Till soul and body sever,
For though all things shall pass away
    His Word shall stand forever.[6]

3. By faith, stay confident in God, even when the situation seems impossible. When Abraham was ninety-nine years old and Sarah, a spry eighty-nine,[7] they were still waiting for the son God had promised them. By this point in their lives, it was humanly impossible for Abraham and Sarah to get pregnant; they were too old! Infertility is terrible for couples who want to have their own children. It means the death of a dream. But for Abraham and Sarah, it was especially a conundrum because years earlier, when Abraham was a youthful and vigorous seventy-five-year-old, God came to him, took Abraham outside into the night, and told him to look up at the stars in the ancient Near Eastern desert sky, saying, "so shall your offspring be" (Genesis 15:5).

This third episode is reviewed in Hebrews 11:11-12 and centers on God's promise to Abraham (which He restates in Genesis 12, 15, and 17) that from him would come a great nation: "By faith Abraham, even though he was past age—and Sarah herself was barren—was enabled to become a father because he considered him faithful who had made the promise. And so from this one man, and he as good as dead, came descendants as numerous as the stars in the sky and as countless as the sand on the seashore" (vv. 11-12).

Think about the number of stars he saw. Can you imagine the look on Abraham's face? I see him beaming with tears in his eyes as he makes the connection between the vast number of stars and the extent of God's promised blessing!

And yet nearly twenty-five long years later, nothing had

changed. The couple was still infertile. Yet they were, at a minimum, realists. They were forced to be. As the years went by, they faced the inescapable reality that they would be permanently childless, apart from divine intervention. Frankly, I take a great deal of comfort in this. This is so like God— putting us in situations way over our head and allowing them to get worse, not better! (And note, just like we tend to do today, Abraham and Sarah grew impatient and at one point took matters into their own hands. Sarah gave Abraham her Egyptian maid, Hagar, and Ishmael was the result. Oh, the pain that sinful union has brought on the planet.)

Yet Abraham remained confident because he knew the character of God. As verse 11 says, Abraham "considered him faithful." So Abraham rested in the Word of God, the promise of God, and ultimately the character of God. And then God appeared to him once more. After reaffirming the covenant He'd made, God said, "No longer will you be called Abram; your name will be Abraham, for I have made you a father of many nations" (Genesis 17:5). Before leaving, God also promised that He would one day reaffirm this same covenant with Abraham and Sarah's son, whom He promised would be born about a year later.

Abraham and Sarah's infertility illustrates an important truth: life can be awfully messy in the middle. By the middle, I mean the period between birth and death. In that middle, Abraham and Sarah waited two and a half decades to receive what God had promised; in the middle, Job's wife told Job to curse God and die, so great was her grief and so deep her agony; in the middle, an unnamed woman, whose story is told in the Gospels, hemorrhaged, bleeding for twelve years straight; and in the middle, another man, mentioned in the Gospel of John, was lame for thirty-eight years.

In the middle today, millions and millions of people never escape poverty, never taste clean drinking water, never get medicine to cure their malaria or hepatitis. Yes, the middle is horrific for many people. It always has been. Here's the thing: the enemy of your soul wants you to believe that the middle lasts forever. But it doesn't! Heaven is what lasts forever for the believer. So with Job, we as believers—up to our eyeballs in the muck and misery of the middle—cry out: "Though he slay me, yet will I hope in him. . . . I know that my Redeemer lives, and that in the end he will stand upon the earth. And after my skin has been destroyed, yet in my flesh I will see God" (Job 13:15; 19:25-26).

The middle is messy, but the messiness of it all doesn't last forever. Abraham knew that, and 1 John 5:4 echoes this same truth: "This is the victory that has overcome the world, even our faith." Faith in the character of God, faith in the plan of God, faith in our future with God. Spiritual confidence leans into God, all of God.

There's an interesting conclusion to this third episode. When Abraham's son of promise was finally born, he and Sarah named their child Isaac, which means "laughter." Go figure. People of faith can laugh at the middle because they recognize that the middle isn't the end—heaven is. Faith always has the last laugh.

4. By faith, sacrifice for God, even when it costs you every-thing. The fourth episode from Abraham's life in Hebrews 11 provides the New Testament's explanation of Abraham's greatest trial. Isaac, the long-awaited, promised son, was now in his teens, maybe his early twenties. Every time Abraham saw Isaac, he was reminded that though God may be slow to fulfill His promises, He is never late! But, then, in what is one of the most unusual commands in the Bible, God asked Abraham to do something unthinkable—to sacrifice Isaac. Hebrews 11:17-19 tells us:

> By faith Abraham, when God tested him, offered Isaac
> as a sacrifice. He who had received the promises was
> about to sacrifice his one and only son, even though
> God had said to him, "It is through Isaac that your
> offspring will be reckoned." Abraham reasoned that
> God could raise the dead, and figuratively speaking,
> he did receive Isaac back from death.

These verses do not deal with the "external" ethical/moral problem of child sacrifice, which was, after all, unilaterally condemned by God in the Old Testament. Rather the focus here is on the "internal" problem: Abraham's faith crisis. Did he believe God enough, did he love and worship God enough, to obey Him? If Isaac, Abraham's son of promise, was to be put to death as commanded by God, how could the promises of God be fulfilled? Ultimately the command raised this question for Abraham: "God, how much of me do You want? How deep do I go?" Abraham was faced, first, with a parental conflict between his love for his only son and his love for God. Second, he was confronted with the spiritual/theological conflict between reconciling the promises of God—"It is through Isaac that your offspring will be reckoned" (Hebrews 11:18)—and the command of God— "take your son . . . sacrifice him" (Genesis 22:2). Ouch!

What was Abraham's solution? He banked his hope on the power of God. Hebrews 11:19 is explicit: "Abraham reasoned that God could raise the dead." Remarkably, prior to the first books of the Bible being written (Job being a possible exception), prior to the doctrine of the Resurrection being laid out in the New Testament (it's only hinted at in the Old Testament), Abraham believed in some sort of personal and bodily resurrection. In fact, the account of Isaac being spared from death became the Old Testament's metaphor for resurrection. Amazing! Abraham's assurance in resurrection, rooted in his confidence in the power of God, may be one of the greatest moments of faith in all of history.

So this final episode teaches us that, when we consciously make sacrifices for God because we are committed to His purposes, He transforms our adversity and anguish into something positive. People who love God and want to please God accept sacrifice.

Sacrifice is saying no to something you prefer so you can say yes to God. It's placing your preferences, what you love, on the altar and telling God, "I want to keep this or have this or do this, but You are speaking to me and I am giving it up. Take it; it's Yours!" In a real and agonizingly difficult way, I had to do that with Carol, and Rhonda had to do that with Tom. We had to give them up. We had to stop clinging. We had to release them to God.

Sacrifice is counterintuitive; it's winning by losing, gaining by giving, living by dying, doing without now so you can be rewarded later in heaven. It's seeing yourself as an alien and stranger in this life. For some, sacrifice means living more simply and downsizing; for others, it's ministering to the poor and the needy, serving when no one notices; it may mean loving and advocating for your handicapped child; it's taking care of the sick, the widow, the orphan; it's staying put in a tough marriage; it's significantly upping what you give of your time, talent, and treasure to the cause of Christ; it's giving up a cherished dream; it's standing up for Christ when others aren't.

Hear me, dear reader: as painful as it is, it's sacrifice that will keep you from wasting your life, because it's sacrifice and service that reveal the lordship of Christ in your life. Isn't this precisely what Jesus was getting at when He said, "If anyone would come after me, he must deny himself and take up his cross and follow me"(Matthew 16:24)? In other words, conversion without immersion in the life of Christ is a perversion of the gospel. And immersion always demands sacrifice. After all, Christ's life was sacrificed; the gospel is inherently sacrificial.

Notice, too, that sacrifice is voluntary. God didn't have to drag Abraham and Isaac to the mountaintop; Abraham went willingly, though sorrowfully. While I might not have had the power to heal Carol, I did have the choice to submit her life to God or to seethe with anger and resentment because He wasn't responding the way I wanted. And many followers of Jesus, when they hear His call on their lives, willingly make uncomfortable sacrifices.

Some years ago when I was in Ethiopia, I got to know a British-trained Ethiopian surgeon, a leader in his large and vibrant evangelical denomination. At the time, he was living seven hours away from his family, seeing them only a couple of weekends a month so he could take care of desperately sick patients and reach people for Christ in a more remote hospital. Frankly, he was the one person who was keeping that hospital going and keeping people alive. This doctor doesn't do that anymore, and certainly, I am not advocating abandoning one's kids, but I was struck by his sacrifice.

More recently and closer to home, my daughter Shannon and her husband, Luke, informed our family that they were moving out of their comfortable townhouse and into a low-rent apartment complex where World Relief resettles international refugees. They planned to join two Wheaton College graduates who were already living there. This way, Shannon and Luke, who are preparing for life as foreign missionaries, could begin to do ministry among the poor. I was okay with this conceptually (I am a pastor, after all!), but when I first walked into the building's courtyard and saw garbage strewn everywhere, screen windows and doors broken, and people from all around the world milling about, I thought, *Oh boy, could I do this?* Since Shannon and Luke moved in three years ago, others have followed. Now they number about ten, including one family with young children, who rented out their house so they could join the intentional community. They tell amazing stories about bringing families and children to church; rushing very sick, non–English speaking immigrants to the hospital; and welcoming people into their little apartment.

Our church is partnering with Greater Europe Mission to reach immigrants in France. As part of this effort, we challenged members of our body to move—in this case, to a town in northern France that is home to a growing number of North Africans. Over the next couple of years, we hope to send ten to thirty people to evangelize and disciple these immigrants. Eight people—three couples and two single men—have already made a three-year minimum commitment to our MOVE Initiative. While it's an exciting opportunity, these people are making huge sacrifices to be part of it.

We love asking our people to sacrifice, to do hard things, in a variety of very different ways, all for the Kingdom of God. Throughout the world, in fact, people of faith are making huge sacrifices for Jesus. Adversity is inevitable—"Man is born to trouble as surely as sparks fly upward" (Job 5:7). We can't avoid trouble, but we can sanctify it by sacrifice. This happens when we surrender our own desires in order to follow Christ and lift Him up here and around the world. "If anyone would come after me, he must deny himself . . ." (Matthew 16:24).

God approved of Abraham, not because he was perfect

or never doubted. (In fact, twice Abraham tried to convince kings that his beautiful wife was his sister so they wouldn't kill him to get to her.) However, as Hebrews 11 makes clear, Abraham's faith in the God who had reached out to him grew stronger as he encountered challenge after challenge. From him, we learn that we will turn adversity on its head when we

- *Obey the call of God, even when we have questions* (v. 8). Abraham's *obedience* wasn't something he conjured up on his own—it was born out of his experience of the living God; it came to life as God supernaturally appeared to him. In other words, Abraham saw the person behind the promises!
- *Wait patiently for the will of God, even when it appears God has forgotten us* (vv. 9-10). Abraham had lapses, but he persevered. His *patience* was rooted in his conviction about the promises of God, which went back to these encounters with God in Genesis.
- *Stay confident in the power of God, even when our circumstances seem impossible* (vv. 11-16). Along the way, Abraham's *confidence* in the faithfulness of God became stronger as he experienced the power, provision, protection, and answered prayers of God.
- *Sacrifice for God, even when it costs us everything* (vv. 17-19). Finally, Abraham's willingness to *sacrifice*, we are told, sprang from his belief in the power of God—specifically, His resurrection power.

Even today, God's followers are called to live with an understanding that, in God's hands, adversity leads to advantage. Remember Karl, the former Air Force chaplain? Though he felt as if God's presence had been withdrawn from him just when he needed it most, he remained convinced that God was present in the midst of his brokenness, and he felt sustained by the prayers of other people. As a result, he caught glimpses of the ways God was using his weakness to advance His Kingdom: "At the nursing home the elderly connect with me because of my disability," he said. "When I roll up to their bedsides, I'm already at their level. I don't have to bend down. 'Karl will understand,' they say as they experience loss of function."

His impact went beyond the walls of that long-term care center. One day he was the speaker at an anointing service for fellow chaplains. After he had delivered his message, the chaplains walked in a line to the front, where Karl was waiting to anoint each of them with oil. As they came forward one by one, they had to stoop down so that Karl could press a few drops of oil to their foreheads. "The first few bent down to the level of my wheelchair," he recalled. "Then one man knelt. Soon they were all kneeling. And perhaps that is what I need to focus on right now. For the rest of my life, through no choice of my own, I'm at the level of one who kneels."[8]

On your knees: there's no better posture from which you can get a peek of how God is working through your own heartache—even on those days when, like Abraham, you don't know where you're headed.

CHAPTER 5

Persevering Faith . . . Jeremiah

I LOVE READING HISTORY, especially the accounts of people who have overcome seemingly insurmountable odds, including some of our American presidents. One of the most colorful and popular was Andrew Jackson, also known as Old Hickory because of his treelike toughness. A decorated general before winning the presidency, Jackson served two terms from 1829 to 1837.

What you may not know is that just weeks before Andrew was born, his father died. When he was thirteen, he and his brother Robert were captured by the British while serving as mounted messengers for the American army during the Revolutionary War. Andrew was struck by a soldier's sword after refusing to clean an officer's boots and was scarred for life. While imprisoned, the brothers came down with smallpox. A short time after their release, Robert died; then quickly, tragedy struck again and Andrew's mother died. Hugh, the oldest of the Jackson brothers, had died almost two years before. So Andrew, or Andy as he was called, was orphaned and all alone in the world by the time he was fourteen. And I think I have problems!

Yet by the 1790s this orphan had overcome his deprivation to become the most successful lawyer in Nashville. When Tennessee became the sixteenth state in 1796, Jackson was elected as its first representative in Congress. Later he became a US senator and a justice of the Tennessee Supreme Court. Rough and tough, he would become famous in battle as a general in the US army during the War of 1812.

But tragedy would strike again. Shortly before he became president at age sixty-two, Rachel, Andrew's beloved wife, died suddenly. Her death came on the heels of a campaign in which both of them were subjected to vicious personal attacks. By the time he took office, Jackson was so weary and grief stricken that some historians tell us he was the saddest president ever to enter the White House. On top of that, President Jackson was racked with tuberculosis most of the time he was in office (which he treated by bleeding himself). Yet this man, who had been through so very much and experienced Job-like disappointment, is remembered as one of America's boldest, most decisive leaders. As Paul Harvey used to say, "And now you know the rest of the story"—and, I would add, the disappointment.

Speaking of tough presidents, Theodore Roosevelt stands almost unparalleled. Made famous in Cuba when he led his Rough Riders up San Juan Hill in the face of stiff and heavy enemy fire, Roosevelt was always an adventurer, climbing the Matterhorn on his honeymoon and embarking on an African safari shortly after leaving the White House.

Though he had enjoyed a privileged upbringing, Roosevelt also had to deal with tragedy early in his life. Four years after he married Alice Lee, she died, shortly after giving birth to their daughter. (His mother died on the same day.) Roosevelt was so grief stricken that he moved out West for two years, leaving his baby daughter in the care of his sister.

While his time in the frontier seemed to restore him, Teddy refused to talk to his daughter Alice about her mother. It was too painful for him. Yet Teddy persevered and went on to become one of America's most admired and respected presidents, serving from 1901 to 1909. After losing a third-party bid for the presidency in 1912, Roosevelt joined an expedition headed into the jungles of Brazil to explore nine hundred miles of an unknown river. His team experienced incredible hardships, including starvation, attacks by the natives, disease, drowning, murder, and the death of three of the party. Roosevelt himself was so sick that he contemplated suicide. The group's adventures were so incredible that their claim to have mapped one of the Amazon's tributaries was received skeptically at the time.[1]

Even more than Jackson's toughness or Roosevelt's spunk, though, I admire the fortitude of Abraham Lincoln.

Lincoln's mother died when he was just ten; that same year, his father moved the family from Kentucky to an area of Indiana that Lincoln would later describe as "a wild region, with many bears and other wild animals still in the woods. . . . There were some schools, so called, but no qualification was ever required of a teacher beyond 'readin', writin', and cipherin'.'"[2]

Two of Lincoln's four sons died in childhood. Eddie was not quite four; Willie, age eleven, died during the height of the Civil War. Compounding his disappointment and certainly not helping his melancholy disposition, President Lincoln had a very difficult marriage. Mary Todd Lincoln was erratic and eccentric, warm but also quarrelsome. (When Mary was judged insane after her husband's assassination, their son Robert had her temporarily committed to a mental hospital that still stands—not too far from my home.)

In his book *Sacred Marriage*, Gary Thomas provides a glimpse into the couple's difficult relationship. For instance, shortly after their marriage, Mary insisted they move from their one-story home to a two-story house, claiming that "everybody who was quality"[3] had one. When Lincoln didn't move fast enough for her, she had a carpenter add a second story while he was away on business. It wasn't only her husband whom Mary would badger. Lincoln paid extra to the family's hired help to keep them on in spite of the stress Mary's temper caused them. The situation didn't improve when they got to the White House:

When a salesman called on the White House
and was treated to Mary's fervid verbal assault,
he marched right up to the Oval Office—those
were different days, to be sure—and proceeded to
complain to President Lincoln about how the first
lady had treated him. Lincoln listened calmly, then
stood and gently said, "You can endure for fifteen
minutes what I have endured for fifteen years."[4]

Lincoln also heard protests from the public about Mary's
spending binges, which included the purchase of hundreds
of pairs of gloves. When her favorite son, Willie, died in
1862, Mary nearly cracked. While dealing with a hysteri-
cal wife—not to mention his own grief—Lincoln was losing
favor among the public as the Civil War dragged on.

In the fall of 1863, Lincoln was asked to make a short speech
at the dedication of a soldiers' cemetery in Pennsylvania. He
wasn't given much time to prepare and then, to top it off, his
son Tad became ill shortly before he was to leave, throwing
Mary into new hysterics. As a result, Lincoln had time only
to jot down a few notes as he left for Pennsylvania. Lincoln
delivered the speech with less-than-usual force, and initially
it was tepidly received. The president considered it a failure.
Author Gary Thomas goes on to say,

But the words were true and genuine, and they
were moving and powerful—and as the newspapers
recorded them without Lincoln's understandable

gloom coloring them, the nation was inspired as never before. The Gettysburg Address is one of the most famous speeches ever delivered on American soil, and those words would eventually be carved in stone, accompanying Lincoln into posterity. It may be a cliché to say this, but it's still true: He shone brightest when his personal life was darkest.[5]

As Thomas considers what enabled Lincoln to persevere through a prolonged war, he notes:

The connection one can make between Lincoln's marriage and his mission is not difficult. It is easy to see how a man who might quit on a difficult marriage would not have the character to hold together a crumbling nation. . . .

"Emancipator" means deliverer from bondage and oppression. Perhaps Lincoln's example can deliver us from the oppression of an empty pursuit of happiness. Perhaps he can set us free from the notion that a difficult marriage will hold us back rather than prepare us for our life's work; maybe he can yet cut us loose from the chains that bind us to the seeking of tension-free lives over the building of lives of meaning and character.[6]

Amazing! Disappointment doesn't need to "hold us back"; instead it can "prepare us for our life's work." It can make us better.

Historians are somewhat unsure of the nature and extent of each of these three presidents' faith. I do know many people are convinced that President Lincoln was a believer. So while each of them is an incredible example of perseverance, there is debate as to what extent they tapped into the strength, hope, and comfort that God provides in the gospel for those who look to Him in times of trouble. Lincoln certainly looked to God.

In the last chapter, we saw how Abraham, by faith, clung to God. In this chapter, I want to look at another example of perseverance in the Old Testament. Once you get the context, I think you'll recognize it as one of the more amazing examples of perseverance in history, let alone the Bible.

Dealing with Disaster

Lamentations, a brief book wedged between Jeremiah and Ezekiel, was written near the end of Old Testament history. Along with the book of Job, Lamentations enjoys the dubious distinction of being one of the saddest books in the Bible. Job is a heart-wrenching story of personal tragedy; Lamentations bemoans a catastrophic national, political, and cultural disaster. As the name suggests, Lamentations is a collection of laments, or expressions of grief, remorse, and agony. It was written by the prophet Jeremiah, who was later called "the weeping prophet" because he grieves so much, particularly in Lamentations, over the fall of Jerusalem and the destruction of Israel. (When I was in Israel recently, a tour guide suggested that Jeremiah might have written Lamentations near the spot where Christ would be crucified centuries later.)

Despite his grief, Jeremiah's faith grew stronger. In fact, I believe faith and perseverance are interconnected. It's one thing to persevere, but another to do so in a way that pleases God. I am biased; as beautiful as the stories of people like Jackson, Roosevelt, and Lincoln are, none compare in God's sight to those who persevere because they believe in God and are absolutely convinced that though He may test them terribly, He loves them deeply. God's Word is clear: "Without faith it is impossible to please God, because anyone who comes to him must believe that he exists and that he rewards those who earnestly seek him" (Hebrews 11:6).

Not only is it impossible to please God without faith, the Bible also tells us that faith is key to perseverance. When we believe, we persevere, we hang tough. Note how James weds the two: "Consider it pure joy . . . whenever you face trials of many kinds, because you know that the testing of your faith develops perseverance" (James 1:2-3). Make no mistake, God had given Jeremiah a challenging and discouraging assignment: to preach to his countrymen, knowing they would not listen. In fact, the Lord told Jeremiah, "Even your brothers and the house of your father, even they have dealt treacherously with you; . . . do not believe them, though they speak friendly words to you" (Jeremiah 12:6, ESV).

There is a cause-and-effect relationship between faith and perseverance. When our faith is stretched, it grows like a muscle in our body. And when our faith grows, our commitment and endurance deepen. In fact, our perseverance will surprise us; it "develops"—to use James's word. Mine certainly has.

Now, let's dig in and look at a stunning example of faith that perseveres and pleases God. As we do, keep in mind that the object of our faith counts more than the amount of our faith.

To put the book of Lamentations in context, it helps to understand that in the book of Jeremiah, which comes right before it, the prophet looks ahead and warns Judah (Israel's southern kingdom) of coming judgment. (Scholars believe parts of Jeremiah were written as early as 627 BC.) In Lamentations, the prophet looks back at the destruction and mourns it.[7]

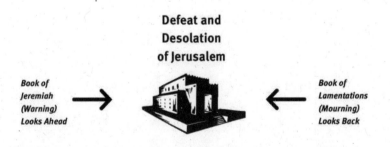

Defeat and Desolation of Jerusalem

Book of Jeremiah (*Warning*) Looks Ahead → ← Book of Lamentations (*Mourning*) Looks Back

Jerusalem, the capital of the southern kingdom, fell to the brutal Babylonians in 586 BC after an approximately two-year siege. The city and the nation were destroyed, its Temple was demolished, and most Jews were deported to Babylon. When we come to the book of Lamentations, Abraham, the father of the nation of Israel, has been dead for about fifteen hundred years; Moses, for one thousand years; and David and Solomon, who ruled during the high point of Jewish national history, for five hundred years. Israel as a nation is now at an end.

Think of it this way: How would you feel if an enemy nation attacked the United States and you were one of the few survivors? Imagine what it would be like if you lived in Washington, DC, and everything there—the White House, the Capitol Building, the Washington Monument, the Smithsonian, the National Cathedral—was reduced to rubble. Think about what you would be thinking and feeling if everyone you knew had been killed or deported. That's Jeremiah in Lamentations. He's beside himself with grief, and he despairs of any sort of future for his country, his people, or himself. To make a bad situation worse, Jeremiah, of all people, knows the situation could have been so different, if Israel had only listened to what God had said through him. Hating the spiritual failure, Jeremiah cries out:

> My eyes fail from weeping,
>   I am in torment within,
> my heart is poured out on the ground
>   because my people are destroyed,
> because children and infants faint
>   in the streets of the city. . . .

The visions of your prophets
    were false and worthless;
they did not expose your sin
    to ward off your captivity.
The oracles they gave you
    were false and misleading.

All who pass your way
    clap their hands at you;
they scoff and shake their heads
    at the Daughter of Jerusalem:
"Is this the city that was called
    the perfection of beauty,
    the joy of the whole earth?" . . .

The LORD has done what he planned;
    he has fulfilled his word,
    which he decreed long ago.
He has overthrown you without pity,
    he has let the enemy gloat over you,
    he has exalted the horn of your foes.
(Lamentations 2:11, 14-15, 17)

Let's be clear. It isn't that Israel had experienced a run of bad luck or that the Babylonians were simply superior militarily; it's so much worse! God finally and unequivocally judged Israel because of her chronic idolatry, disobedience, unbelief, and sin.

However, as we come to chapter 3, astonishingly, Jeremiah's mood changes. Here, in one of the most transcendent sections in literature, Jeremiah records a beautiful expression of faith, which is all the more incredible in light of the pervasive desolation and destruction all around him. Look at his familiar words:

> Yet this I call to mind
>   and therefore I have hope:
>
> Because of the LORD's great love we are not consumed,
>   for his compassions never fail.
> They are new every morning;
>   great is your faithfulness.
> I say to myself, "The LORD is my portion;
>   therefore I will wait for him."
>
> The LORD is good to those whose hope is in him,
>   to the one who seeks him;
> it is good to wait quietly
>   for the salvation of the LORD. . . .
>
> For men are not cast off
>   by the Lord forever.
> Though he brings grief, he will show compassion,
>   so great is his unfailing love.
> For he does not willingly bring affliction
>   or grief to the children of men. . . .

Is it not from the mouth of the Most High
    that both calamities and good things come?
Why should any living man complain
    when punished for his sins?

Let us examine our ways and test them,
    and let us return to the LORD.
(Lamentations 3:21-26, 31-33, 38-40)

Five Features of Persevering Faith

In the ashes of the cancer and death of Carol, certain passages were lifelines for me; they kept me from sinking. Lamentations 3 was one of them. In it I found five characteristics of extraordinary faith.

1. *Clarity* about the character of God. Extraordinary faith is clarity about the character of God. Theological clarity means that you know God and you know that you know God! It's conviction born in a vision of God. You aren't arrogant; but on the other hand, you're not fuzzy about who God is. This is found in verses 21-23:

Yet this I call to mind
    and therefore I have hope:

Because of the LORD's great love we are not consumed,
    for his compassions never fail.

They are new every morning;
 great is your faithfulness.

Think about these words. Perhaps Jeremiah writes them just after walking by the bodies or the mass graves of dead Jews, some whom he had known for years. Or maybe he is sitting among the ruins of the Temple, weeping. He says in effect, "Yes, the loss is total and horrific. But there is a deeper reality I cling to. You see, I believe God isn't just loving, I believe God's love is *great*—above and beyond anything we can fathom. Further, I believe that God isn't just compassionate. I know His compassions *never fail*; that is, there will never be a time when they end. Great is His faithfulness."

Now we might be tempted to reply, "Excuse me; what did you say, Jeremiah? What fruit drink have you been sipping?"

"No, no, no," I hear Jeremiah responding. "Take your eyes off the circumstances. See the deeper plan, the deeper purposes, and the power of God here. There is no pit so deep that God's love, compassion, faithfulness, and sovereignty are not deeper still, including the pit of the destruction of the Jewish nation."

So Jeremiah concludes verse 24 with the assertion, "The LORD is my portion." In other words, God is his priority, his lifeline, and his life. God is everything to Jeremiah, his all in all and his rock. Yes, God must judge Israel because of her sin, but Jeremiah believes that, regardless of how bad Israel's circumstances, they will never negate the character and the promises of God.

Jeremiah's clarity about the character of God—His great love, compassion, faithfulness, sovereignty (sovereignty is just one of the many implications of the word *portion*)—is here in verses 21-24. Be honest: if you were in his circumstances, would you be so staggered, so buried under the weight of your own personal despair that seeing the character of God by faith would be impossible? I know many of us might be! Yet this vision of God is what makes Jeremiah unshakable. No wonder he perseveres; no wonder he overcomes insurmountable odds. My friend, what you believe about God is the most important thing about you.

The hardest thing I had to do during Carol's illness was to tell twelve-year-old Ryan that his mother would die. His older sisters knew it; Ryan didn't. Just after the medical team told me that Carol was too weak for more treatments and that it was time for her to go home to hospice care, I took Ryan to Portillo's, a restaurant near the Chicago hospital where she was being treated.

Amazingly, I was okay, but I wanted Ryan to be okay too. I didn't want him to impale himself on the horns of bitterness and unbelief. So I decided to be straightforward, answer any questions I could, and assure him we would be okay as a family. I prayed, trusted God, and Ryan responded well in that horrible moment. I carried him on my shoulders as God was carrying me on His.

My faith in God's goodness and love was my safety net, and it kept me out of the abyss of anger and unbelief. It became Ryan's safety net too. I can't begin to describe the faithfulness of God; the net was secure though the bottom fell out. Three days after my conversation with Ryan, Carol died.

Do you see why I say that what you believe about God deep down in your soul can make you or break you? Let me ask you some questions that I ask myself.

- Do you really believe God loves you like Jeremiah believed God loved him—even though his circumstances screamed just the opposite?
- Whether you're in the midst of month after despairing month of a job loss; in the seemingly unending dark night of family, financial, or health problems; in the aftermath of horrific chronic sexual or emotional abuse; or when no one seems to understand you and you feel so very alone—do you really believe, at the core of your being, that God is faithful, like Jeremiah believed that God is faithful? Do you believe God cares about you?

God never asks for just a part of you; He never even asks for most of you; He demands all of you. From the beginning to the end of the Bible, we discover that the people of God who are clear about the character of God are the ones who give themselves completely to Him. And when the bottom falls out, they still stand.

2. *Dependence* on the faithful character of God. Don't misunderstand—faith isn't just a head thing. We don't just

check a box that says "I believe." In the New International Version, the first clause of Lamentations 3:25 reads, "The LORD is good to those whose *hope* is in him"; the New Living Translation says "to those who *depend* on him" (emphases added). One translation uses *hope*; the other, *depend*.

Let's consider why that is and its significance to this second point. Over the years, Wheaton Bible Church has been the church home of a number of highly gifted Old and New Testament scholars who have helped produce major English translations of the Bible. I've heard them return from translation committee meetings and talk about spending hours, not on just a few verses, but on a few words!

They would tell you that in Lamentations 3:25, *hope* and *depend* are correct translations of the same Hebrew word. The semantic range here allows for both and illustrates the Jewish and biblical perspective that "to hope" is "to depend" and "to depend" is "to hope."

But it's different for us today. When we say "I hope so," we mean, "Maybe yes, maybe no." So we say, "I hope it isn't going to rain today," even though five minutes later it may be raining. No big deal; we meant "maybe."

Biblical hope, Jeremiah's hope, however, is different. It isn't iffy or uncertain; it's a confident expectation and assurance (something, sadly, we Cubs fans have lacked for most of the last one hundred years!). It's *certainty* rooted in the goodness of God.

This kind of hope or dependence transforms everything in you and about you. It fuels a faith like Joshua's, that dares to pray that the sun will stand still, or like David's, that dares to take on Goliath, or like Peter's, that gets out of the boat and walks on water. This dependence always leads to action. (Not surprisingly, in every illustration of faith in Hebrews 11, there is a corresponding action—genuine faith always acts.)

So the difference between the first and second meanings is that of believing a surgeon is good and letting him do surgery. Dependence—that is, saving or biblical faith—is saying yes to the surgeon; it's depending on him to "save" you. When it comes to trouble or discouragement, dependence means more than assenting to the facts that God is loving and sovereign. It means acting in light of those truths.

Jeremiah was as tough as nails, definitely a man's man, but he was also one of those rare men who could say, "I'm not perfect, the people around me certainly aren't perfect, but I know that God is fond of me, He loves me, He's going to be good to me. So I choose to focus on and depend on the goodness of God, not on my dismal circumstances." Tender heart; tough hide.

I don't know how you can say, "I believe the Lord is good" as Jeremiah does in verse 25 and not say, "God, here I am. Take my time, my treasure, and my talents. Please use them, even when I am bleeding, that others may experience Your goodness." Biblical hope, Jeremiah-like hope, leads to total surrender that follows total dependence.

3. Unquenchable *passion* for God. In the second half of verse 25, after Jeremiah has said, as we saw above, "The Lord is good," he finishes his thought by adding "to the one who seeks him." The verb *seeks* is active, and in the Hebrew it conveys the idea of examining, inquiring, looking, searching. It's seeking God until you find Him, rest in Him, and sense His presence. Jeremiah and David shared this burning passion for God. Their significant leadership responsibilities and constant adversity never quenched their flaming hearts.

Centuries earlier David described it this way:

O God, you are my God,
    earnestly I seek you;
my soul thirsts for you,
    my body longs for you,
in a dry and weary land
    where there is no water.
(Psalm 63:1)

Notice that David begins by stating his governing reality—"O God, you are my God"—and follows that with his passionate response—"I seek"; "my soul thirsts"; "my body longs." Seeking God means you run to Him like a little child runs to his or her parent. But you do it repeatedly, not because you have to but because you get to, you want to, you are in love with your heavenly Father. You want to be with Him. Seeking God means you look for God and stop to listen to Him. You long to hear His voice and be held by Him. You want to go where He goes; you long to value what He values and hate what He hates; you want to be taken care of by Him. You want more and more of Him, even if, like Jeremiah, you are surrounded by people who have had enough of God and want less of Him. Not you—you run to God . . . you seek Him.

You may be underemployed, underchallenged, short on money and long on time; or you may be overemployed with precious little time. Maybe you are married; perhaps you are single. You may be healthy and active, or sick and struggling. Regardless of your circumstances, my prayer for you is that God will give you the grace to seek Him and to run after Him. In Lamentations 3:21, Jeremiah gives us a specific picture of what this looks like when he says,

> Yet this I call to mind
> and therefore I have hope.

When Jeremiah says, "this I call to mind," isn't he referring to other promises of God as revealed in Old Testament Scripture? To the ways God demonstrated His love to Israel in the past? Isn't he thinking of God's faithfulness to Abraham, Moses, Joshua, and David? Isn't he revealing that a person who seeks God is a person who loves the Word of God? He or she takes the time to process, to digest, and to be formed by the truths of God as revealed in His Word.

Now look at verse 55:

> I called on your name, O LORD,
> from the depths of the pit.

Doesn't this mean that the person who seeks God is the person who prays, never stopping no matter how bad it gets? You could argue that most of Jeremiah's adult life and ministry were spent in the "pit," yet regardless of how great the crisis, Jeremiah kept pleading and agonizing with God, asking Him to make good on His promises and seeking forgiveness for the sins of the nation.

The second half of Lamentations 3 is a dramatic illustration of a man marked by his humility before God, his willingness to confess sin and repent, and his openness toward God that enables him to express his frustration with God yet still accept God's sovereignty when everything around him crashes and burns.

May God give us the grace to run and keep running to Him!

4. Total *submission* to the plan of God. In verses 26-32, Jeremiah writes:

> It is good to wait quietly
>   for the salvation of the LORD.
> It is good for a man to bear the yoke
>   while he is young.
>
> Let him sit alone in silence,
>   for the LORD has laid it on him.
> Let him bury his face in the dust—
>   there may yet be hope.

Let him offer his cheek to one who would strike him,
and let him be filled with disgrace.

For men are not cast off
by the Lord forever.
Though he brings grief, he will show compassion,
so great is his unfailing love.

Notice the words *wait quietly* in the first line of this passage. Now jump down a bit and check out the word *silence*. Why does Jeremiah talk about quiet and silence? I think these two words picture something important—a refusal to complain! They picture the acceptance of God's assignment when the assignment is terribly difficult. They reflect humility and a staunch determination not to dishonor God with one's lips, even during times of great trauma.

These words bring to mind the image of a believer fighting to get to a place of submission, like a soldier who says, "yes sir" and refuses to complain, even when he doesn't like his orders. Or the child who refuses to argue with a parent who is over the top and wrong. It's the spouse who bites her tongue and waits until the timing is right before gently correcting her husband. Of course, the deeper the pain, the deeper and more prolonged our faith and refusal to complain, the more God is glorified.

When Kristin Richard married Lance Armstrong in 1998, she gave up her job in public relations and moved with him to Europe so he could focus on his cycling career. Lance went on to win the Tour de France five times during their marriage. In the meantime, Kristin reveled in her role as stay-at-home mom to the couple's three children, a son and twin daughters.

Most outsiders assumed they had a near-perfect marriage, so when news of their divorce broke in 2003, many people were stunned. Kristin herself said she felt like a failure. "The biggest thing for me . . . was the idea that I had failed my children. I failed in marriage and then, bigger than that, I failed my kids, because to me what I wanted to show them is what unconditional love looks like. And to me, unconditional love is represented by an intact family."[8]

Yet as a Christian, Kristin's faith became her lifeline and, for the first time, she understood the value of silence.

It's easy to lose sight of God when life is sweet and easy, but there is something awesome about despair, and it is the closeness of God when we are at our weakest. With my pride stripped down, and my mind open and alert, suddenly I had eyes to see and ears to hear. I learned how to stop when I didn't know the next move, instead of forging blindly ahead. I learned to ask for direction, and then heed that advice. I learned it is OK to pause, to breathe, to not know, to say nothing.[9]

If I could do one thing over in life, I would complain less. I think sometimes we as evangelicals pride ourselves on not complaining when things are going well—that is, when there is precious little to complain about! But somehow we think it's okay to complain when things aren't going well because, of course, from our perspective the situation warrants it. Be honest here—think about all the complaining we evangelicals do about politics alone. We complain about the weather (especially those of us who live in Chicago), our sports teams, our kids' teachers, our neighbors, and sadly, our churches. I am so burdened about this in my own life that I recently memorized some verses in Proverbs to help me check my complaining tongue. One of my favorites is this one:

> Even a fool is thought wise if he keeps silent,
>   and discerning if he holds his tongue. (Proverbs 17:28)[10]

But let me say something else. Along with a refusal to complain, Jeremiah demonstrates a rugged perseverance, a second aspect to his submission:

> Though he brings grief, he will show compassion,
>   so great is his unfailing love. (Lamentations 3:32)

This verse is a theological feast! God ordains our grief; He "brings" it. He is sovereign over our good times and our bad times. God permits what He hates in order to accomplish what He loves. Submission means stopping ourselves from self-pity, whining, and complaining. We keep on keeping on.

We persevere. It means when we are facing trouble we don't become consumed with "why me?"

As I mentioned earlier, one of the best things I have done in this ordeal is to refuse to ask that question. (I talk about this a lot because as a pastor I see all sorts of people impale themselves on the pointed tip of this question, and too many, unfortunately, never fully recover.) We are way ahead of the game when we ask, "God, what do You want me to learn about You? How can I grow?" That requires keeping our eyes on God, not on our circumstances.

In addition, Jeremiah displays remarkable and rugged patience:

> Let him bury his face in the dust—
>   there may yet be hope.
> Let him offer his cheek to one who would strike him,
>   and let him be filled with disgrace.
>
> For men are not cast off
>   by the Lord forever. (Lamentations 3:29-31)

"Let him bury his face in the dust"; that is, lie down in the dirt and stay there (which was an Old Testament form of discipline—doesn't it also sound like an appropriate method for today's teenagers and husbands?). And then, "Let him offer his cheek to one who would strike him"; that is, let him endure punishment. Both suggest we should be okay with pain, adversity, upheaval, and not getting our own way—even if it's not "fair." This is not meant to advocate a defeated or self-loathing spirit, but one that is teachable and patient. We should be more willing for God to *conform* us than for God to *comfort* us because we are in submission to Him. And the fruit of submission is patience. If you are easily offended, you haven't learned to deny yourself.

I am not a patient man. I can hear my kids laughing as I write this, "Boy, is that true." But the Holy Spirit gave me incredible patience with Carol's illness. I marvel at how easy it was for me to remain patient. I have learned that sometimes it's easier to be patient in the more extreme, "out of control" situations than in the regular, ongoing limitations and annoyances of life. But God wants us to be patient in all situations: "Be joyful in hope, patient in affliction" (Romans 12:12); "Help the weak, be patient with everyone" (1 Thessalonians 5:14); "You too, be patient and stand firm, because the Lord's coming is near" (James 5:8); "The Lord is not slow in keeping his promise. . . . He is patient" (2 Peter 3:9).

By teaching me, an impatient man, to learn submission, adversity and discouragement have helped transform me and make me more like Christ.

5. Complete *obedience* to God. I love Lamentations 3:40:

Let us examine our ways and test them,
     and let us return to the LORD.

Extraordinary faith is evidenced by complete obedience to God. I'm not talking about perfection; none of us are perfect (even though some of us in the church pretend otherwise). Instead, God's Word here teaches us that obedient people hate sin and are truly sorry for it. They confess, they repent, they return to God after they have blown it, again and again. Christians are people who "return to the LORD" throughout the course of their lives. They want to live the new life in Jesus Christ, not the old life of sin. They want to prove in their experiences that they are new creatures in Christ (see 2 Corinthians 5:17).

Obedient people aren't perfect, but they understand that stress isn't an excuse for anger; that adversity doesn't issue them a rain check so they can put off holiness and grace; that busyness doesn't earn them an exemption from God's Word; and that loneliness is not a justification for sexual immorality or pornography.

"Let us return to the LORD." Obedient people aren't just moved by stories about people like Jeremiah; they say, "By God's grace I am going to be a Jeremiah in this situation." Obedience isn't optional; the fruits of the Spirit aren't optional; sharing Christ with lost people isn't optional; and giving of our time, talents, and treasure to do hard things for the Kingdom isn't optional either. We "examine our ways"— our weaknesses, our shortcomings, and our sins. We bring them to the light, and if we need help—and many of us do—we get help.

As Jeremiah discovered, perseverance is possible only

when we are clear about God's character, dependent on His faithfulness, passionate about our relationship with Him, completely submitted to His plan, and committed to obey Him. The same is true today. So are the benefits of living like this. As Tony Snow said, "The challenges that make our hearts leap and stomachs churn invariably strengthen our faith and grant measures of wisdom and joy we would not experience otherwise."[11]

God invites you to surrender yourself totally to Him, to trust Him, to love Him. Jeremiah's words of amazing faith in Lamentations 3 changed my life at its darkest point. May Jeremiah's faith be your faith!

CHAPTER 6

Good Grief

LIKE MANY EIGHTH-GRADE BOYS, Matt Anderson loved sports like soccer and basketball that pushed him to his physical limits. So clearly something was wrong when, during a soccer match, Matt asked to be taken out of play because he had no energy. In fact, he'd been fighting a low-grade fever and fatigue for a while. The following day, Matt and his family were given the diagnosis: he had leukemia.

For the next several years, Matt clung to the verse "Be strong and courageous" (Joshua 1:9) as he underwent intense chemotherapy treatments. He completed his freshman and sophomore years and was one of the "honored heroes" at the 2008 Leukemia & Lymphoma Society's Light the Night Walk for Chicago. Still, the disease continued its assault.

Matt's unique type of leukemia had created too many other problems for his once vibrant and healthy body to handle. So severe were his complications, so steep his descent, that not only was he in a medically induced state of unconsciousness during the last few weeks of his life, he also had to be transferred from one leading hospital to another that specialized in stabilizing the particular problems in his lungs and heart. Three years after beginning his fight, Matt died.

I conducted Matt's funeral, an amazing celebration of a young man and a young family who were deeply committed to honoring Christ in their divinely appointed trial. Matt's parents, Mark and Jill, had remained strong during the long ordeal. As an illustration of this family's profound commitment to each other, Mark never let his son spend a single night alone. Mark was there every night, all night—all 286 of them—that Matt spent at a hospital. Yes, Mark had a job that enabled him to do this, and yes, Jill had three other younger children who demanded her attention, but this dad's commitment to Matt and his knowledge of his son's disease and complex treatments were beautiful to behold. I wasn't surprised that an unusually high number of Matt's medical caregivers came to his funeral. They had been impacted by watching Matt and his family, who deeply loved Jesus and each other.

A couple of days before the funeral, I sat in Mark and Jill's home talking with them about their grief and a few issues related to the funeral. God had burdened me to ask Mark to speak at the service, and he agreed. Suddenly, though, as we were talking, I couldn't speak. All I could do was cry. Mark and Jill understood. You see, the Andersons had been our neighbors. Matt, my son, Ryan, and a whole slew of kids grew up playing all sorts of games, including lots of baseball in the retention area between our two houses. So as I sat in Mark and Jill's family room that afternoon, I could see the corner of my old house—the house in which Carol had died—out their back windows. Frankly, it was suddenly all too much for me. First Carol, now Matt—and we had lived just a couple of houses apart. It seemed so wrong, so sad. I had come to minister to the Andersons in their grief; yet now I was overcome by my own grief. Boy, did I feel like a loser of a pastor!

We spent the first part of this book considering how people who are convinced of God's faithfulness and love prevail despite great difficulty and sorrow. No matter how strong our faith, however, we must not lose sight of this: disappointment and loss inevitably lead to grief and feelings of disequilibrium. And as I learned at the Andersons' home, we may be pummeled by grief when we least expect it.

So while in chapters 2 through 5, I focused on biblical truths we as Christ followers can cling to in difficulty, in this chapter and the next I will deal with the critical companions of disappointment—grief and change. Both are inevitable, regardless of the strength of our faith. You will be way ahead of the game if you are aware of these two friends.

Waves of Grief

In our church, death sometimes seems to come in waves. What I mean is that there may be a period of "calm" when we almost forget about this ever-present reality. Then all of the sudden, seemingly out of nowhere, we are hit with a number of deaths, like uninvited guests who have crashed our party to steal our joy. These losses become waves that we are powerless to stop. We go from one death to another, sometimes just days apart. When that happens, our already busy staff is sent scrambling, and honestly, because we care so much for our people, we end up mourning and grieving right alongside our church families. During those days our staff meetings and Tuesday morning staff prayer times become very sober. A cloud descends for a while.

For a year or so, starting in 2009, the death waves came crashing again. There was Barry, the lay leader of our men's ministry and a key part of our worship ministry. Then we lost Mike, a father of fifteen- and eleven-year-old daughters, to pancreatitis. Mike had been active in our Africa ministry and was married to a woman on our staff. Less than six months after joining our worship and technical production team, Steve was riding his bike to work at the church when he suffered a massive heart attack and died. Then, of course, there was Matt, struck down during what would have been his junior year of high school. And there were others, all devastating losses, all so sad.

Barry, Mike, Steve, and Matt all left behind grieving

families whom we wanted to rally around. And while each of these situations was different—as they were from my situation and from yours—I've discovered certain principles seem to be universal when it comes to grief and loss.

This chapter focuses on the emotional side of mourning; that is, the visceral response to the difficult and lengthy process of incorporating a painful new reality into our lives. How can any good come out of grief? In this chapter, we'll explore why grief is an unavoidable companion when we've suffered a significant loss; we'll also consider the ways people typically respond to someone who is grieving, taking care to distinguish what is helpful from what is unhelpful (even though probably well-intended).

Grief is inevitable

Grief is real, grief is deep, and at times grief can be overwhelming. Yet some people say that faith and grief don't mix. They suggest that the stronger our faith, the less time we will waste on grief.

But hold on! How do we account for the grief Joseph displayed at the death of his father (see Genesis 50)? What about David's intense grief as he mourned the death of his son Absalom (see 2 Samuel 18–19)? Doesn't Jesus Himself say, "Blessed are those who mourn, for they will be comforted" (Matthew 5:4)?

What was the point of the Old and New Testament practice of expressing grief with sackcloth and ashes? Wasn't it a vivid cultural display of the depths of bereavement, not to mention repentance? Sackcloth and ashes illustrated that death was deeply, publicly, and demonstrably grieved. And such grief was normal and rational.

Ray Mitsch and Lynn Brookside, authors of *Grieving the Loss of Someone You Love*, a daily devotional I personally found helpful, explain our inclination to pretend we can sidestep grief—as well as why that is unwise:

> Naturally, our sorrow is uncomfortable. Most of us would rather not have to endure it. Some of us are so anxious to avoid it that we seek scriptural grounds for doing so. We decide that since we can't control death we can at least control our feelings about it. We try to prop up our feeble efforts to short-circuit our pain by saying we are being "people of faith." But people of faith accept God's will for their lives. They allow themselves to experience the feelings that God has given them, because it was God who created us with the ability to feel our emotions— even our pain.[1]

Grief is profound

When a spouse or close family member dies, or when someone goes through a divorce, the survivor hasn't lost just a spouse, or a family member, or a marriage. He or she has lost so much more! To say, "I am sorry for the loss of your wife," is not saying enough. It fails to do justice to the totality of the trauma, to the other losses involved. For example, when Carol died I lost my confidant, my counselor, my companion, my soul mate, the emotional center of our family, the family organizer and coordinator. Carol paid our bills, did our laundry, cleaned our house, bought our groceries, loved on and directed our children, and kept our busy social calendar together. She was the person I longed to be with more than any other.

Perhaps that is why I identified with this comment from Peter, a man who was profiled in the book *Widower: When Men Are Left Alone*:

> When the surgeon told me Sherry was dying, I felt he had given *me* a death sentence. It wasn't Sherry dying, but *me*. My identity had become so entwined with hers that I didn't experience any separation from her. I cried for three days before I recognized it was *she* who was dying, not me.[2]

Peter vividly illustrates just how pervasive the loss of a spouse can be. As a result of what I have been through, I no longer tell people they will get over a major loss. I understand firsthand they probably won't and that is okay. They will get better and get through it, but not over it. Nor will I tell anyone "time will heal," as if grief is merely an illness. There are certain things that time does not heal. It's so much more complicated because grieving is a complicated process, full of fits and starts, ups and downs—panic followed by moments of surprising, profound calm.

I was struck by some facts with which the authors of *Widower* begin their book:

There are more than twelve million widowed people in the United States. Each year, for every three women who are experiencing the loss of a mate, two men experience the same loss—creating nearly a quarter of a million new widowers every year.

Until recently, not very much has been known of what happens to these men, but if you have lately joined their number, this much we can tell you:

- *Your chances of being killed in a car accident have increased 300 percent.*
- *Your chances of committing suicide have increased 400 percent.*
- *Your chances of dying from heart disease have increased 600 percent.*
- *Your chances of dying from a stroke have increased 1000 percent.*[3]

They point out that losing a spouse is at the top of the list of life's most stressful events; indeed, it's the event against which all other stressful events are measured. No wonder, then, that the loss of a spouse places increased stress on a person's immunological system, which explains the increased susceptibility to illness—as well as psychological and medical problems later on if the widower doesn't deal appropriately with his grief.

It is more than the fact that you have lost a friend and companion and mate, more than the fact that you are now single in a coupled society, more than the fact that you have lost a caretaker and social connector.

It is also the fact that you have been brought to the very brink of the Mystery, and then you have been left behind.[4]

Are you feeling better?

Grief is disorienting

In the first moments of a crisis, when people are reeling from a loss, they are numb, disoriented, and unable to process much, if anything at all. I will never forget sitting in the emergency room with Barry's wife about an hour after her forty-three-year-old husband died suddenly and unexpectedly following a workout. Through her tears she kept repeating, "I don't know how I am going to make it. I don't know what to do." Such can be the shock to the system.

So what did I do? I just listened, stayed quiet, and ever so gently said, "I am so sorry. Take one hour at a time; then one day at a time. I have done this; you can do this. God will see you through." The truth is, in such a moment no one really knows what to say or do, and sometimes the grieving are convinced, temporarily, they will not make it. I certainly felt that way at times.

Yet this numbness often continues for a long period of time, extending into the weeks and months that follow a trauma or significant disappointment. People reeling from a significant loss may be forgetful; they may zone out for periods of time; or they may have trouble remembering the little things, like where their keys are. I experienced all of this, and I specifically remember the scary thought of getting out of the car several times, thinking, *I don't remember a single thing about driving here.*

Perhaps that explains why the practical ministries extended to my family when we had been thrown off course by Carol's illness were so precious. My friend Steve cut my grass week after week. Dan kept our older cars and anything mechanical running. Chuck and his wife, Pat, prayed and prayed and, endearingly, when he called, Chuck would often get too choked up to talk. I loved that because it revealed such a tender, caring heart.

Jeff basically ran our house, keeping track of our kids and paying all our bills. Brian organized a lot of our travel plans back and forth to Houston, giving or securing for us numerous airline miles. (He was always frustrated when he couldn't get Carol a seat in business class.) Scott and Mark rearranged their schedules to make sure I never worked out alone when I was in town. (Scott, a former Marine fighter pilot, did get annoying by continuing to press me to go hard in our workouts when I was tempted just to feel sorry for myself.)

Jim, the chairman of our church's elder board, came to Houston the most. On the day when Hurricane Rita was about to crash into Houston, Jim and I laughed like crazy as we made a mad dash for the airport before it closed. It's a wonder we made it there on time—the interstate was like a parking lot as everyone from the Texas coastal area seemed to be fleeing north at the same time. Carol didn't quite share our humor.

Every pastor does ministry a little bit differently. I have always done ministry in the context of friendships—some especially close. When tragedy struck our family, my investment in friendship paid dividends way beyond anything I could have imagined. Just as Aaron and Hur held up Moses' hands during a critical battle, strengthening him to depend on God (Exodus 17), my friends held me up and made my tragedy bearable. It takes a village—or better, the village called the body of Christ—to do cancer, divorce, job loss, or death. I know.

Grieving Together

But how do you know whom to allow to get close to you during your period of grieving? Or how do you minister most effectively to a friend or loved one whose heart is breaking? Having been both a caregiver and a care receiver, I offer some observations and suggestions.

Listen with the heart

First, don't speak; just listen. That's an overstatement, but it makes an important point, especially in the first moments of a crisis. Don't forget that severe pain shuts down people's ability to cope and process things, at least for a period of time. Those friends who remember this will be most helpful because they will be sensitive. They will speak less and listen more.

My friends, almost to a person, did that with me, both as Carol's sickness progressed and after her death. Several of them flew to Houston at various times to sit with me at the hospital during Carol's surgery and with us during appointments. Yes, we chatted some, but mostly they just listened and gave me a wonderful gift—the ministry of their presence. Other friends kept in touch when we were home. They asked good questions, never pressing but always present.

While they offered their presence, these friends didn't try to offer a ministry of providing answers. I didn't need answers. I needed support. They knew that. They also understood: (1) often there aren't answers, certainly not specific ones, and (2) some pain is just too deep for words. So they listened a lot and spoke less. And today, in part because of my friends, I am still standing.

Speak from the heart

Of course, there is a time and a place to speak to a hurting friend. When you do speak, however, the best thing you can say is "I'm sorry." But mean it—don't say it glibly. Before I went through my trial, I tended to fixate on coming up with nuggets of wisdom to dispense to those who were hurting. After all, isn't that what pastors do? Now, though, I recognize that when I'm speaking to people who are mourning, it's not just their minds that are floundering, their hearts are breaking.

When tragedy struck my family, the people who ministered best to me were those who spoke to my heart. Normally I love it when people speak to my mind; I love a well-written, insightful book. But after Carol died, I wanted to be with people who were not afraid to acknowledge my loss.

Sympathy is feeling with the feelings others feel (e. g., "I'm so sorry about _____"); empathy is understanding how another feels (e. g., "You must really be _____"). When you are sympathetic, you feel *for* someone. When you are empathetic, you feel *with* that person. Empathy goes deeper, it seems. It is the capacity to identify with, to participate in another's pain and express deeper insight because you've been there or because you at least feel it deeply. Because of my own experiences, I seek to extend lots of empathy (understanding) laced with significant doses of sympathy (feeling) to grieving people.

As a result of the economic meltdown over the past few years, I have been with more people than ever before whose financial world has been turned upside down after losing their jobs. These are good people now unemployed after decades in the marketplace. Because our church has a fairly active ministry to those who have experienced divorce, I also talk regularly to people who are groping in the darkness of divorce and trying to piece their lives back together in a way that pleases God. Many of these men and women feel just awful. You can see it in their eyes.

Whether I'm speaking to someone who is unemployed or someone who has just gone through a divorce, what I say has changed since losing Carol. Now I find myself saying things that express my sorrow, like "This must be awful," "I can't imagine how difficult this is," and sometimes just plain old "Ugh." Don't misunderstand, I will give people advice, and I will strongly state what a biblical response to disappointment looks like if and when it is needed. However, I do that only after I've really listened and expressed words of empathy.

Because a few well-meaning people said some less than helpful things to me after my wife's death, I now warn people facing major disappointment and loss that those who try to comfort them often won't know what to say. Though their intentions are good, they may say some things that only prove they didn't know what to say! Like the guy who came up to me on a Sunday morning just a few months following Carol's death. After about two months away from the pulpit, I had just resumed preaching. As I stood in front, he came up to me and said, "Rob, I know what you are going through as a single parent because my wife was out of town this weekend and I had the kids by myself. Man, was it hard!"

Now what do you say to a well-intentioned but grossly inept remark like that—comparing the death of a wife to a wife gone on a retreat for two nights? Thankfully, I was so stunned all I could say was "yeah" before walking away. But to be honest, did I ever feel alone and misunderstood! This young man had touched a nerve, and tears quickly filled my eyes.

Then there was a well-meaning man who said to my son just days after his mom died, "Boy, Ryan, I hope you don't move."

Ryan turned to me and said, "Dad, are we going to have to move now too?" I won't tell you how that made me feel, but I will tell you that the last thing that Ryan needed was additional instability. My purpose isn't to blast people, but to make the point that it's always easy to open our mouth and insert foot, but especially when people are raw. Be careful.

In contrast, what a blessing are words that convey empathy and understanding. I am struck by the word *aptly*, as used in Proverbs 25:11: "A word aptly spoken is like apples of gold in settings of silver."

Aptly suggests a variety of things: words that are gentle, or appropriate (including age-appropriate), or powerful, or concise and clarifying, or pleasant. Apt expressions for me were statements like one my mother, also a single parent, made when she told me, "Rob, you can do this. It will be tough, but you will make it." Or the ones from friends who said, "Carol was extraordinary. I'm going to miss her, and I was just her friend. I hate this for you." I also appreciated when others told me, "I don't know what to say but, man, I will pray."

Aptly also suggests timely, though, so be careful of your timing. When I was in seminary, Howard Hendricks, one of my professors, used to say, "Men, never discuss money with your wife after ten o'clock at night." His point was timing. So is mine.

Weigh your words

That leads me to my third suggestion. Be careful about what you say, spiritually. Unless asked, don't preach. There are a couple of aspects to this. For starters, be cautious about making theological pronouncements. Granted, statements like, "God will use this for good," "God works all things together for good," and even more innocuous ones like "The angels are rejoicing now" or "Your loss is heaven's gain" may all be wonderfully true. However, most people in severe trauma are not in the place to receive such statements, which may sound like heartless platitudes.

Personally, this led me to be very careful about what I said to my kids after Carol's death. I know that God works all things together for good, but in terms of my four kids, it's still hard to see how the loss of a godly mother like Carol is good. To be sure, we all see glimmers of insight now and one day we will see clearly, but today is not that day. I never want to reduce the death of a parent or a child, the agony of a divorce, or the horrific experience of abuse to a theological statement. Nor do I want to insensitively pin this on God in a way that would build resentment in a young mind.

Whatever you do, avoid advancing any form of the cheap and hurtful theology of extreme faith healing, which is closely aligned with the prosperity gospel. It's man-centered theology at its worst. By far the most difficult thing spiritually for both my friend Tom and for Carol during their illnesses was the gentle suggestion by a few people that if they had more faith they would be healed.

One day Tom asked me for help in interpreting the message of a booklet he was given about Joel Osteen's mother, who wrote about being healed of cancer because of her faith. It is quite a dramatic story. But, boy, did it discourage Tom. I can still see the pain in his spiritually tender eyes as he asked, "Are they right? Am I lacking faith? Is my cancer my fault? How do I respond to this?"

Something similar happened to Carol when another pastor told me he knew Carol would be healed because she was a woman of faith. He sent us some literature to prepare us for God's blessing, all activated of course, by the strength of Carol's faith. I will not go into all the many weaknesses of the "name it–claim it" approach to the Kingdom, nor will I point out all its significant theological inadequacies and half-truths. Instead consider these words from Randy Alcorn's book *If God Is Good*.

> In an "it's all about me" world, we don't accept answers that entail our inconvenience, much less our suffering and death. We assume faith healing or medical breakthroughs can eliminate suffering and cure all diseases.
>
> According to prosperity theology, we can declare our way out of disease. Pastor Joel Osteen writes, "Maybe Alzheimer's disease runs in your family genes, but don't succumb to it. Instead, say every day, 'My mind is alert. I have clarity of thought. I have a good memory. Every cell in my body is

increasing and getting healthier.' If you'll rise up in your authority, you can be the one to put a stop to the negative things in your family line. . . . Start boldly declaring, 'God is restoring health unto me. I am getting better every day in every way.'"[5]

Do you see the problem? Such thinking puts God in the role of servant, not master! So God exists to serve us, to make us healthy and happy, not to be our Lord. Yes, He has some rules, but if we follow them then we can have what we want—material success and physical health. All we have to do is declare it, and God becomes a genie or our "personal shopper."[6] This is a distortion of the gospel. In *Christless Christianity*, Michael Horton points out that prosperity theology sees neither condemnation for our failure to follow God's righteous law nor any justification:

> Instead of either message, there is an upbeat moralism that is somewhere in the middle: Do your best, follow the instructions I give you, and God will make your life successful. . . . God is a buddy or partner who exists primarily to make us happy.[7]

Then Horton explains why that is so contrary to the gospel:

> Jesus and the apostles clearly proclaimed the total depravity of the human heart and redemption by

Christ alone through faith alone. . . . It was Jesus who said that anyone who does not trust in him "stands condemned already" (John 3:18 NIV). That was because for Jesus, the judgment he came to save us from by enduring it for us had God and his glory, not me and my temporal happiness, as its reference point. The ditch we had dug for ourselves was so deep that only God incarnate could pull us out of it by falling in and climbing back out of it himself as our Substitute and Victor. For Osteen, the good news is that on judgment day God will look at our heart. According to Scripture, that is actually the bad news. The good news is that for all who are in Christ, God looks on the heart, life, death and resurrection of his Son and declares us righteous in him. It is not a cheap gift, but it is a free gift.[8]

Is it any wonder, then, that such teaching totally misses the centrality and beauty of pain, suffering, and loss in God's plan of discipleship for His children? In addition, it overlooks the huge price (deprivation, imprisonment, death) the persecuted church is paying right now in different parts of the world for following Christ. It misses this because it trades the Kingdom dream for the American dream. But, worse, it completely misses the divinely appointed role of suffering in the life of our Savior: "Although he was a son, he learned obedience from what he suffered" (Hebrews 5:8).

Alcorn says:

> Of course we should seek to be healthy, both
> physically and mentally. But we miss out on a great
> deal if we fail to see God can also accomplish his
> purposes when we lose our health and he chooses
> not to heal us. . . .
>
> After a terminal diagnosis, many people spend all
> the remainder of their lives searching for a scientific
> cure or a spiritual healing, or both. I don't, of course,
> fault sick people for seeking a cure! But . . . we
> should focus our energies not simply on *avoiding*
> death, but on investing our time in *preparing* for it—
> getting right with God and ministering to others.
>
> Let me share some bad news: I have a fatal
> disease. I'm terminal. I'm going to die. But the news
> gets even worse. *You* have the same fatal disease—
> mortality. You're going to die too.
>
> Nothing could be more obvious. Yet somehow we
> don't take it to heart, do we?[9]

Many people are susceptible to false teaching that leaves
them wondering if their failure to be healed could be the
result of their own unbelief. This includes sick but spiritually sensitive people like Tom and Carol, who went into
temporary emotional tailspins at this thought. Briefly, and
I could see it in their faces, Tom and Carol wondered if
they were displeasing to God, spiritually weak, and—more

damaging still—if their horrible diseases were somehow their fault. Their questions were not surprising—they were raw, stripped, losing family and all that life offers, but mostly they were unusually spiritually sensitive. And spiritually sensitive people are always open to whatever God has for them. They are acutely aware that they could believe more, pray more, fast more. I mean, who among us couldn't?

Fortunately, Tom and Carol quickly saw the fallacy of this kind of thinking, realizing that it ignores the fact that faith is a gift. Consider how wrong and self-destructive this focus is—instead of focusing on God and His love, faith healing demands you focus on self and what you must do. Is there one more button I can press? Tea leaves I can try? Something else I can do? All this is rather difficult when your mind is full of chemo and all sorts of other drugs and your body is racked with pain.

There's one other type of statement to be cautious about making to a grieving person: be very careful about interpreting God's will. Remember that you may or may not be correct. Several people who loved Carol and me told us they believed God was telling them Carol would be healed. Sometimes they said God had given them verses as confirmation!

I'm not suggesting that God never leads one of His children today in a particular matter. I do believe God can speak to us, leading and guiding us as His children in specific and remarkable ways. Sometimes we are conscious of this direction; sometimes not. Over the years I have learned the hard way, however, that there is often a difference between my impression of God's will—sometimes even my impressions of what He is saying to me through a passage in His Word—and how God's will actually plays out in the circumstances of our lives. I believe God's Word alone is sufficient and complete, final and authoritative. God's Word is infallible, not my interpretation of it.

The difficulty, of course, is that trying to determine whether we have heard from God about a particular situation is subjective. Often you and I really don't know for sure whether God was speaking to us about a situation or whether the tacos we ate the night before had some strange effects on us. So be cautious about telling someone what God is telling you about them—whether it's about an adult child returning to the Lord, an unemployed friend getting a new job, a wayward spouse returning home, or an ill family member being healed of a terminal illness. Hold loosely what you think God is saying. You, of course, mean well, but if you turn out to be wrong, you could possibly hurt the very person you intend to help, by creating false hope.

For example, one Sunday Carol and I stood in the front of the church auditorium talking to people after a service. A woman came up to us and told us that she was sorry about Carol's cancer but wanted us to know that she was convinced Carol would be healed. God had told her. Later Carol asked me, "Do you think she is right? What do you think, Rob?" Such a scenario happened more than once.

But let me be candid. I had a similar experience. Every couple of years I slowly read through the Psalms, especially when I am hurting. One morning when Carol was ill, I was reading Psalm 30. Then I came to verse 2—"O LORD my God, I called to you for help and you healed me."

My world stopped at these divinely inspired words of David. Suddenly, I had a powerful sense that God was telling me through this particular verse that Carol would be healed. Or perhaps it would be more accurate to say I had a sense that God might be saying something to me. I also knew from the get-go that my impression could be wrong so I held it loosely, testing it over time. I was aware that the verse didn't say, "Carol will be healed" but that David "was healed" and that there is a difference between my sense of an application of a text and the context of the text. To be honest, I understood the difference immediately, and I wondered whether I had had that feeling simply because I was so raw and I so wanted Carol to be healed. I talked to her about this in depth, and she told me she had had a similar experience with a verse. As it turned out, both our "senses" of God's voice (our application of His Word) were wrong in this particular case.

Here's my point. Listen to God; let Him speak to you. Long for Him to speak to you. But remember that while His written Word is infallible, we may be mistaken about what He might be telling us now about a particular situation. Remembering that will help you be careful about telling others what you think God may be saying to you as well. Let God be God; never box Him in and please be careful about announcing His will.

Just be there

Fourth, err on the side of being there for people who are grieving. Don't disappear, don't fail to call, don't stop checking in.
Be present, not absent. I know what you may be thinking
because I hear this a lot when I talk about this point. You
don't want to intrude; frankly, you don't know what to do.
My counsel to you is to do something, almost anything, and
along the way ask your traumatized friends what they want.
Err on the side of involvement. When appropriate, ask them
if they need space; let them set the parameters for you. But,
as much as possible, keep showing up.

If you are the one grieving, let people in; let them do
things for you. Right after Carol died, my sister flew in from
Oklahoma City and spent a week or so at our house, helping,
listening, doing whatever she saw that needed to be done.
She just came and got involved. Actually, she did it a couple
of times. It was huge. My cousin Marilyn stepped in and ran
tons of errands for me—and she always seemed to find amazing bargains. My younger brother, Randy, helped by getting
me over a financial hump. His generosity was incredible.

I hate to admit this, but I really blew it here once.
Seriously. And that may be an understatement. Shortly after
my friend Tom died, I disappeared on his wife, Rhonda! Yes,
we sold our boat together, and yes, I called her a couple of
times. But Tom was my close friend, and I had been over at
his house all the time when he was sick.

In many ways, though, I seemed to check out on her. To

be honest, I wanted to be cautious about the male–female thing. (I tend to be very cautious about that, and Rhonda is an attractive woman.) In addition, less than four months after Tom died, Carol was diagnosed, so almost immediately our own lives changed dramatically. But here's the deal. Rhonda felt deserted by her pastor, by her husband's best friend. She found herself wondering, *Where is Rob? Doesn't he care?* I shudder to think how many other people I have hurt through such neglect because I either subconsciously or consciously thought, *I'm just too busy. After all, this is a large church.* Hurting people long for sensitive, meaningful personal touches, for help (as I illustrated with examples of what my friends did for us), and for empathetic conversation.

Embrace the tension

Next, accept and, as appropriate, remind others of the tension I mentioned in the book's introduction. On the one hand, whatever has happened to cause grief is awful, irretrievable, and a game changer. Don't deny the pain, don't pretend it isn't bad or awful. Christians, of all people, should never lapse into denial.

For instance, if you or a friend is grieving because one of you was a victim of sexual abuse, denying or minimizing the horrific nature of what happened, especially when done by the people closest to the victim, is terribly isolating. Frankly, sexual abuse is one of the worst pains there is. The violence, guilt, betrayal, and stigma it brings is beyond words. Not surprisingly, people who have been abused have a desperate longing for empathy. Theirs is an especially dark world. They long for us to say, "This is horrific. I don't know what to say; I can't imagine. I am so, so sorry."

So grieve with, weep with, and comfort those who are hurting—not just the abused, but your teenager, when he misses the game-winning shot, bombs an important test, or is rejected by a friend. Grieve with the young adults around you who have had a miscarriage or who can't get pregnant. (My oldest daughter's first miscarriage was on Mother's Day, three years after her mother had died.) Grieve, as we have in our extended family, with an aging parent whose beloved spouse has descended into the oblivion of Alzheimer's, never to return again. Isn't this what the apostle Paul meant when he said to "weep with those who weep" (Romans 12:15, ESV)?

Yet that's only part of the story. The tension comes because while horrendous things happen, God is still wonderfully and totally sovereign (see Psalm 103:19; Ephesians 1:11). Believe it and gently point people to this truth, when appropriate. Making God's sovereignty a dominant reality in our lives is our main protection against hopelessness.

Don't hesitate to point to God's control, but don't be glib about it either. I knew God was in control of Carol's situation, but more often than not, I needed empathy, not instruction. Furthermore, one just has to go to the massive slum Kibera in Nairobi or to the garbage dumps and impoverished villages of Central America to get the distinct sense that life is unfair. Life appears so very unjust, but it is not random. Believers in Africa and Central America would be the first to tell you that their conviction about the sovereignty of their heavenly Father provides an insurmountable wall of protection around their hearts. It is, in a real sense, their lifeline of hope. The same can be true for us when we live with this tension between the seeming unfairness of suffering and the sovereignty of God. Invite your grieving friends to embrace it too. Few things will help them more. It's not an "either-or"; it's a "both-and." It's not "either suffering or sovereignty" but "suffering and an infinitely just God"!

Whether you are hurting or are reaching out to someone who is grieving, point to God's promises when things seem darkest. Believer, never forget that

- God has our name etched in the palms of His hands. (Isaiah 49:16)
- He is our rock. (Psalm 18:2, 31, 46)
- He is always present. (Psalm 23:4)
- He is in control of our lives. (Psalm 103:19; Romans 8:28)
- Though there are some 100 billion stars in our Milky Way galaxy alone, God calls every star by name. (Psalm 147:4)
- Not even a sparrow falls to the ground apart from God's plan. (Matthew 10:29)

- So intimate is His knowledge of us that God knows every thought as we form it (Psalm 139:2) and every word before we speak it (Psalm 139:4).
- God even knows the number of hairs on our head (Matthew 10:30)—and we lose over a hundred a day.

God has your back! Gently remind yourself and others of God's sovereignty, not as a club to clobber those less believing, but as a balm to heal the wounded. Pray and ask the Holy Spirit to help you know when to remind people of these truths.

Distinguish temporary assignments from eternal ones

Finally, remind people, as you are able, of the sufficiency of Christ. I am a proponent of the growing family ministry movement in evangelical churches today. Our church is deeply committed to helping parents make their homes discipleship centers. Many would say that at a human level, next to the church, nothing is more important than the family. I love my family, and my kids know it. However, I would quickly add that, at the divine level, family is always second. Jesus Christ is primary, and we must avoid making the family an idol. We should avoid letting our comfort (what's more comfortable than being part of a good family?) keep us from God's global purposes and the obedience of discipleship (again, this is not an "either-or").

So also marriage is temporary according to Jesus (Matthew 22:30); in addition, some people will never marry or have a family (which is one reason God has given us the church). If we're not clear on that, we will never let our kids do hard things, dangerous things for Jesus that might cost them their lives—like living, ministering, and accepting challenging assignments in very difficult places around the world. I know my perspective is colored; I have learned that just a few out-of-control radical cells in the human body can dramatically alter family life. But I also wonder if we understand how temporary and fragile many of these things really are, including our deepest and most profound relationships.

When you understand that come hell or high water, Jesus is first and transcendent above all things, all structures, all relationships; that His lordship over your short life is total and absolute; and when you lovingly and gently communicate that message to people in pain, you have the potential to help them enormously by showing them what ultimately matters. So I have said to people in the aftermath of a painful divorce, "The bad news is your marriage failed; the good news is Jesus Christ, not your marriage, is primary in your life." Grieving parents, like Mark and Jill Anderson, understand that their child is now in the wonderful presence of Jesus and that Jesus somehow will sustain them and that they *will* continue to serve Him.

As you work through your own grief, may God give you the grace to embrace His instruction:

Let us fix our eyes on Jesus, the author and perfecter of our faith, who for the joy set before him endured the cross, scorning its shame, and sat down at the right hand of the throne of God. Consider him who endured such opposition from sinful men, so that you will not grow weary and lose heart. (Hebrews 12:2-3)

CHAPTER 7

The Challenge of Change

ABOUT TWO MONTHS into Carol's melanoma treatments, I was hit by a sobering and disturbing thought. I was getting ready for bed one night in the hospital's hotel room in Houston, a long way from home. It had been a disconcerting day. Outside the fall weather was beautiful, but Carol and I were each sequestered in separate grim rooms deep in the interior of one of our country's largest cancer facilities. We were surrounded by very ill people.

Alone in my room, the awful realization suddenly hit me: like it or not, the stimulating, in-depth conversations about life, ministry, marriage, our feelings, and our kids that Carol and I had always enjoyed were in the past. For twenty-six years, our joyful humor and banter had consistently energized our relationship and family life. It had deepened the emotional, spiritual, and physical intimacy we had thrived on. All of that was gone, forever. All of it had been stolen by thousands of minuscule, out-of-whack cells that had invaded Carol's body like a thief in the night and were now robbing her of life. Like a ship suddenly taking on water, Carol's body was engulfed by an unusual cancer. At the same time, the disease had brutally and almost instantly pushed aside the normal things of our fairly routine but beautiful life together. We were sinking.

And I knew then and there that I wasn't going to get her back, ever. I could no longer talk to Carol about lots of things. I was losing my best friend. Worse, I had this growing sense that I would have to start functioning as a single parent before I would become one. Carol was still very much alive, but I was now alone in ways I had never anticipated or thought possible. She was in the hospital; I was across the street in the hotel. We were together, but we were separating. That was a dark moment for me. I got down on my knees beside my bed and begged God for mercy.

As we explored in the last chapter, when we've experienced great loss, grief is unavoidable. We'll explore yet another common struggle in this chapter: change—which is often an uninvited, unimagined, and overlooked consequence of life's biggest challenges. Being a disciple of Jesus Christ means you don't waste sorrow and you don't waste change. That night in the hotel room, I was beginning to comprehend the magnitude of the upheaval our family faced.

Cancer, especially an aggressive one like Carol's, brings so many changes. For example, there's a dramatic loss of energy for the patient, brought on not just by the disease itself but also by the potential cure; that is, the radiation and the chemotherapy. So difficult are these treatments that the adage "the cure is worse than the disease" often smacked of understatement to us. Just getting through the day was a huge deal. In addition, over time, Carol, like others, developed what is sometimes called a "chemo mind," a blurring and slowing of thought, brought on by the potent and difficult chemotherapy medicines.

Another change was the constant, overwhelming information overload. Just keeping the medicines straight was a huge challenge, especially the drugs that counteracted the side effects of other meds. Even the medical staff would occasionally mess them up, never doing anything major or life-threatening to be sure, but occasionally missing a round of one set of meds or offering another that was no longer okay. Frankly, it was a complex process for the medical staff because Carol was on so many potent and dangerous drugs! She had a rare cancer, which meant there was not a cut-and-dried medical protocol. Reading between the lines, I realized that also meant little had worked, ever. Two or three times, just as we were getting familiar with one treatment regimen, we were shifted to another.

Along the way, various doctors, all experts in their field, suggested different treatment options, and nonmedical people weighed in as well, trying to help ("Have you heard about Canadian green tea leaves?"). We had to learn complex terms, treatment regimens, and technical information. And we had to make quick decisions while continually being told nothing was certain. Three or four times we had to rush to the emergency room in the middle of the night to figure out why Carol's temperature was spiking or why a rash was suddenly breaking out. Cancer totally changed our lives.

Change—like a forced march to a destination you would never choose—is an inevitable result of disappointment, especially a major setback. Cancer, our disappointment, set in motion changes that will affect our family for the rest of our lives.

But the opposite is also true. Disappointment is the result of change. Change is both a cause and a consequence of disappointment; change breeds disappointment and disappointment breeds change. Because they are so closely related, it's important to consider exactly what change is, how we handle it, and the important psychological and spiritual transition necessary for dealing well with it.

Some Things Never Change

First, however, I need to clarify something important: I am speaking here about personal change, situational change, and organizational change (our church's relocation has been a huge organizational change). I am not, however, talking about theological change. The distinction is important. Let me explain.

Spiritual health, according to God's Word, is a function

of being clear that the gospel is Christ alone, grace alone, faith alone. This is Ephesians 2:1-10. The church is the pillar, support, and servant of this sacred truth. This truth is revealed. It is fixed, constant, and transcendent. It supersedes cultures, languages, politics, people groups. Eras and egos. In a word, it is unchanging. In America today, though, change is the air we breathe. Every day, it seems, we see change on so many different fronts—technological, social, and political, to name just a few. We're continuously pushed to be open-minded and tolerant of change. And since we want to be "humble" (God calls us to humility, after all), doesn't it make sense to be open to theological change, particularly when we are wrestling with troubling questions in the midst of difficulty?

Absolutely not! The problem comes when we view humility, not as the opposite of pride, but as the opposite of having definite convictions. This is tolerance on steroids; tolerance taken to an unhealthy extreme. I am all for humility, but when it is equated with uncertainty, with relativism, and an "anything goes" attitude, it becomes both wrong and dangerous. I don't want any part of that.

Here's why: God has spoken clearly, plainly, and intelligently in His Word, and He has given us ears to hear His voice, eyes to read the Bible, and minds to understand it. So while we are to be humble relative to ourselves—our gifts, abilities, and life situations—we dare not be humble (that is, uncertain or doubtful) about the core Christian beliefs. Doubt yourself, for sure, but trust the gospel, trust God, trust His Word, and yes, trust your biblical convictions. Never confuse humility with uncertainty.

A century ago, G. K. Chesterton, in his usual humorous but pointed way, anticipated this problem:

> Modesty has moved from the organ of ambition . . . [and] settled upon the organ of conviction, where it was never meant to be. A man was to be doubtful about himself, but undoubting about the truth; this has been exactly reversed. We are on the road to producing a race of men too mentally modest to believe in the multiplication table.[1]

If the riveting New Testament book of Acts teaches us anything, it is that vibrant churches and Christ followers aren't obnoxious and insensitive, and they certainly aren't rigid and hard-hearted. On the other hand, they never compromise either their message or their theological convictions, regardless of cultural pressures or their circumstances. In fact, preaching a particular and narrow gospel—often to a hostile crowd—was central to the success of the early church.

So please listen to me: Change is good. God is in the business of change; it is inherent in the gospel. His divinely ordained rescue operation brings salvation, followed by sanctification and ultimately glorification. I, for one, can't wait for the new heaven and new earth. The changes, all of them, are enormous. Therefore, as God's people we must be open to all sorts of change, especially spiritual change in repentance and growth. And when life seems to throw dramatic and gut-wrenching change at us out of nowhere, Christ will give us the strength to hold our heads up, even when our hearts are heavy. But let's be careful, as we undergo change, not to capitulate, to soften, to reduce, or to water down God's Word or our theological convictions. Let's not confuse personal change with theological change.[2]

Epic Change

Not only is the Word of God unchanging, it includes invaluable insights into how we can successfully navigate change. The Old Testament book of Joshua, for instance, is a magnificent historical journal that chronicles one of the most memorable nation-state changes in all of history. It is the divinely inspired record of the Jewish conquest of the land of Canaan under the leadership of Joshua.

Remember that God promised Abraham in Genesis 12 that He would bless him with descendants who one day would have a land of their own where they would flourish and be the source of worldwide blessing. This promise would find its most breathtaking and momentous fulfillment in the advent of Christ, the promised Messiah, though Israel still awaits its final completion. The book of Joshua is significant because it details how God fulfilled His promise to give Abraham's descendants their Promised Land, not quite six hundred years after God made His covenantal promise to Abraham. The divine side of this—God's transcendent purposes and plans—is that God's timing may not be our timing, and God's ways may be very different than our ways, but God always keeps His Word.

So we read in Joshua 1:1-5:

> After the death of Moses the servant of the LORD, the LORD said to Joshua son of Nun, Moses' aide: "Moses my servant is dead. Now then, you and all these people, get ready to cross the Jordan River into the land I am about to give to them—to the Israelites. I will give you every place where you set your foot, as I promised Moses. Your territory will extend from the desert to Lebanon, and from the great river, the Euphrates—all the Hittite country— to the Great Sea on the west. No one will be able to stand up against you all the days of your life. As I was with Moses, so I will be with you; I will never leave you nor forsake you."

I love it when God says, "No one will be able to stand up against you." God is promising divine protection, divine power, and (as He states in the second half of the verse) divine presence. Taken together, this entire passage illustrates the sovereignty, control, and authority of God. Israel was about to undergo one of the most significant and colorful changes in all of history. God knew that if the Israelites were going to thrive as they left the wilderness, they had to remember that God keeps His promises, God protects, God doesn't abandon

His people, and God would see them through. Those same promises apply to His followers today.

As I've said, after years of pastoral ministry, I have concluded that a key difference between Christ followers who transcend their circumstances and those who don't is that, before crisis ever hits, the first group is deeply passionate about their faith and deeply rooted in the Word, while the second considers faith just one more good thing in their lives. As a result, when difficulty comes, the first group focuses on and lives in light of the divine realities of life, while the other is unable to do so. Here on the threshold of the Promised Land, after six hundred long years, God was calling Israel to prioritize their faith life; He was directing them to live vertically, not horizontally.

When we face our challenges, we can take refuge in the divine side of change, the fact that God is in control. But we must also navigate the human side, the bewildering adjustments and new decisions we must make. So Israel had to make the long march through the wilderness and then fight many battles to secure the land that had been promised to them long before. The map on the next page offers a geographical picture of Israel's movement from Egypt through its wilderness wanderings to the edge of the Jordan River, where the events of Joshua 1 begin. It's a map of the route of the Exodus.

There are three geographical phases:

1. **Egypt:** The Israelites were in bondage here for 430 years (see Exodus 12:40). Their history as slaves in Egypt is described in the first half of the book of Exodus.

2. Wilderness: Because of the Israelites' inability to handle spiritual change, they wandered in the Sinai Peninsula for forty years (see Deuteronomy 8:2, 4). Their time in the wilderness, which went on much longer than necessary, is described in Numbers and Deuteronomy.

3. The Promised Land: When we come to Joshua 1, Israel is camped near the upper right hand corner of the map,

on the east side of the Jordan River opposite Jericho. They are waiting for God's command to cross the Jordan and take the Promised Land.

Let's return to Joshua 1, as God continues speaking to Joshua:

> "Be strong and courageous, because you will lead these people to inherit the land I swore to their forefathers to give them. Be strong and very courageous. Be careful to obey all the law my servant Moses gave you; do not turn from it to the right or to the left, that you may be successful wherever you go. Do not let this Book of the Law depart from your mouth; meditate on it day and night, so that you may be careful to do everything written in it. Then you will be prosperous and successful. Have I not commanded you? Be strong and courageous. Do not be terrified; do not be discouraged, for the LORD your God will be with you wherever you go."
>
> So Joshua ordered the officers of the people: "Go through the camp and tell the people, 'Get your supplies ready. Three days from now you will cross the Jordan here to go in and take possession of the land the LORD your God is giving you for your own.'" (vv. 6-11)

Three times in these verses, God repeats His command to be strong and courageous. Why three times? Because people were going to die, taking the Promised Land was going to be difficult, and it required war. The book of Joshua outlines Israel's struggles against thirty enemy armies, and unless Israel was prepared spiritually, it wouldn't happen. I am sobered by this. God's assignments are always right, but the bigger ones are never easy. This assignment God was giving Israel, at least to many of the Israelites and probably at times even to Joshua, was scary-hard. When God said in verse 9, "Do not be terrified," He was encouraging Joshua to remember the divine side to the struggle while acknowledging that the human side would not be easy, it would be terrifying.

Now let's consider what Joshua 1 teaches us about the subject of change. How should we think about it biblically?

Change is hard

First, change can be hard—disorienting, destabilizing, and discouraging—because it forces us into the unfamiliar, into risk. Even good change like Israel's move into the Promised Land required that. Look more closely at the language of verse 9:

> Have I not commanded you? Be strong and courageous. Do not be terrified; do not be discouraged, for the LORD your God will be with you wherever you go.

Notice that God wasn't telling them they should eradicate their fear (which would have been impossible); He was telling them to overcome their fear (which would be possible if they trusted Him). Also consider God's timing: He spoke to His people as they were transitioning from a respected leader (Moses) to his successor (Joshua); from living as nomads to occupying their own land.

Years ago when I did my doctoral work in the area of change, I had no idea it would become such a big part of my life. One of the benefits of my study was learning the distinctions between change and transitions. In fact, experts will tell you that it's not change that's so hard; it's transition. William Bridges, in his book *Managing Transitions: Making the Most of Change*, addresses this at the corporate level, but I've discovered that the principles apply at the personal level as well. I have savored his insights below for years:

> Change is not the same as transition. *Change* is situational: the new site, the new boss, the new team roles, the new policy. *Transition* is the psychological process people go through to come to terms with the new situation. Change is external, transition is internal. . . .
>
> Unless *transition* occurs, *change* will not work. . . .
>
> When we talk about change, we naturally focus on the outcome that the change will produce. If you move from California to New York City, the change

is crossing the country and learning your way around the Big Apple. . . .

Transition is different. The starting point for transition is not the outcome but the ending that you will have to make to leave the old situation behind. Situational change hinges on the new thing, but psychological transition depends on letting go of the old reality and the old identity you had before the change took place.[3]

Do you see the difference? Change is an outcome; transition is a process. Carol's diagnosis was a change in our circumstances; my struggle in the hotel room was transition—the beginning of my letting go of the life I had built with Carol, one that I dearly loved.

Transition starts with an ending—paradoxical but true. Test this fact in your own experience. Think of a big change in your life: your first managerial job, or the birth of your first child, or the move to a new house. Good changes, all of them, but as transitions, each one started with an ending.

With the job, you may have had to let go of your old peer group. They weren't peers anymore, and the kind of work you liked may have come to an end. Perhaps you had to give up the feeling of competence that came from doing that work. . . .

With the baby, you probably had to let go of

regular sleep, extra money, time alone with your spouse, and the spontaneity of going somewhere when the two of you felt like it. Here, too, your sense of competence may have come to an end as you found yourself unable to get the baby to eat or sleep or stop crying.

With the move, a whole network of relationships ended. Even if you kept in touch, it was never the same again. . . .

Even in these "good" changes, there are transitions that begin with having to let go of something. There are endings. There are losses. I'm not trying to be discouraging—just realistic.[4]

Bridges then explains that the biggest problem that we encounter during transitions is "the failure to identify and be ready for endings and losses"[5] that change produces.

The same is true at an individual level for you and me, and it was also true for Israel back in the day! Go back to Joshua 1 and look at verses 6-10 again. When God keeps repeating, "Be strong and courageous," He's acknowledging the psychological and spiritual aspects of transition. God is teaching Joshua something you don't want to miss: don't be unrealistic about change, don't deny the difficulty, but don't fear it. God wasn't telling Joshua that he would have no fear, confusion, frustration, or anxiety. God was saying, "Don't give in to your fear. Trust Me."

Students of transition, like Bridges, have pointed out this

psychological transition involves a threefold process: (1) the ending, losing, letting go; (2) the neutral zone; and (3) the new beginning.[6]

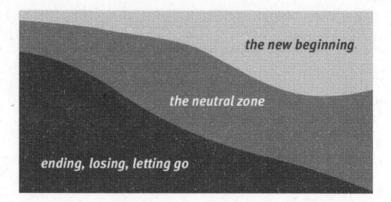

Each of these segments fits one of the geographic phases we considered earlier:

1. The Ending (Egypt): The process of leaving what is familiar and comfortable.

2. The Neutral Zone (the wilderness): The unsettling in-between time when you know change is coming but you don't yet know how you will land.

3. The New Beginning (the Promised Land): The period of developing a new identity and renewed sense of purpose as realignment sets in.

If you're like me, you've experienced several difficult transitions in life. One of the most vivid examples for me occurred after my grandmother on my father's side died when I was in my thirties. My grandmother was an extraordinarily loving woman—an almost "perfect" grandmother. I remember walking into her picturesque backyard one last time and sitting down on a beautiful, white antique wrought-iron bench that circled a large tree. I had sat on that bench countless times while growing up, and now I was thinking, *It's over. I will never be here again.*

Located just a couple of miles from the house where I grew up, her big house had a really big, rolling backyard that ended right on the banks of St. Joe River in northern Indiana. The yard had a beautiful rose garden, a tennis court, and a creek on one side. It was "paradise" for us as kids. Growing up, my brother, sister, and I spent long, lazy summers swimming, fishing, and water-skiing. We'd head back down on cold winter days to ice-skate. When I was in my early teens, I felt as if I ruled that river. Now it was over, like a vacation you never wanted to end. I was profoundly sad. And I was experiencing an ending.

I faced a more horrible ending and transition as I was losing my ability to communicate with Carol. That's what's so very hard about cancer, divorce, job loss, or death. Endings are hard. Interestingly, Egypt was a bad place for Israel, a place of bondage and torture, yet Israel wanted to return to Egypt; that's the strength of the pull of the familiar and the past; it's made more potent when coupled with the fear of the unfamiliar and the future. Change is like that—it's very difficult.

I've alluded to another ending our church experienced when we relocated from downtown Wheaton, Illinois, a location that had served us exceptionally well for almost eighty years. The thought of leaving our campus—with its neighborhood, its proximity to Wheaton College, plus the hardly insignificant fact that Starbucks was within walking distance—saddened many good people within our church. Endings are sad—even good endings like moving to a brand-new and much larger campus just about seven miles away.

As I explained these concepts to our church shortly before we moved, an amazing thing happened—it took the pressure off! Acknowledging the sorrow inherent in a significant ending gave us permission to be sad, which helped ease our pain. Our ending meant we were leaving a place that was familiar and full of wonderful spiritual memories. This was the place that many of our members had come to Christ, met and married their spouses, been baptized, or heard from God.

Shortly before we relocated, I said to my son, who was thirteen at the time, "Ryan, you should think about getting baptized."

He said, "I think I am finally ready, Dad."

To that I responded, "Great, buddy. You can be a part of the first baptisms at our new church!"

His response stunned me: "Oh, Dad," he retorted, "I want to get baptized at the old church. I feel so comfortable there."

So it's not just older people who are "traditionalists," who want things to stay the same; thirteen-year-olds feel that way too. Why? Change is hard, so as God commands Israel, we must believe. With Jesus we say, "Not my will . . ."

As our church began making preparations to relocate, a number of people were really upset with me because we dared to move. I deeply believe that one reason we, even as Christ followers, get so bent out of shape over change is because we confuse change with transition and fail to acknowledge the important role that anger or sadness plays as part of an ending and the disequilibrium that is naturally part of the neutral zone.

Seeing Bridges' chart helped our congregation understand that this threefold process is normal, necessary, and natural. It also helped us relax as we came to understand the importance of "the neutral zone"—that time of adjustment and adaptation. For many, navigating the neutral zone was quick and easy; for others, it was slow and difficult. This in-between time can be unsettling because the outcome is not yet clear. It is a time of letting go, which creates disequilibrium and chaos at multiple levels. It's scary.

To make this point, Bridges quotes another author:

It is not so much that we are afraid of change
or so in love with the old ways, but it's that
place in between that we fear. . . . It's like being
caught between trapezes. It's Linus when his
blanket is in the dryer. There's nothing to hold
on to.[7]

Only when you've acknowledged and worked through the ending and transition can you fully engage with the new beginning, the new future. This is the time to develop a new identity and a renewed sense of purpose.

When you face disappointment and the changes that your pain, loss, and adversity bring, you, too, will go through this threefold transition—that is, if you are to transition well. It's the caterpillar-to-cocoon-to-butterfly (or childhood-to-adolescence-to-adulthood) rhythm of life, of change.

But here's the point—we do ourselves and others a huge disservice if all we do is focus on the new beginning and fail to acknowledge the anger, the fear, and the sorrow of endings, as well as the confusion, stress, and disequilibrium of the neutral zone. All are normal components of change. Shakespeare once quipped: "How poor are they who have not patience! What wound did ever heal but by degrees?"[8]

Bridges states it this way:

> Most organizations . . . pay no attention to endings,
> don't acknowledge the neutral zone (and try to avoid
> it), and do nothing to help people make a fresh,
> new beginning, even as they trumpet the changes.
> Then they wonder why their people have so much
> difficulty with change.[9]

Change requires faith

Once you recognize that change and transition are hard, don't forget the second truth, one that is particularly important to followers of Christ: effective change requires faith. Lots of faith. Deep faith. Rock-solid faith!

Three times God commanded Israel to be "strong and courageous" (Joshua 1:6, 7, 9). Essentially He was telling them, "You don't breeze your way through change; you believe your way." You can't breeze your way because change is difficult; you believe your way because you know God is faithful.

Job expressed this dichotomy when he cried out: "Though he slay me, yet will I hope in him" (Job 13:15). David flipped conventional wisdom on its head by affirming, "Even though I walk through the valley of the shadow of death, I will fear no evil, for you are with me; your rod and your staff, they comfort me" (Psalm 23:4).

Over and over the Bible reminds us that our heavenly Father is faithful. The writer of Hebrews builds his argument on the faithfulness of God when he exhorts:

> Since we have confidence to enter the Most Holy Place
> by the blood of Jesus, . . . let us draw near to God with
> a sincere heart in full assurance of faith, having our
> hearts sprinkled to cleanse us from a guilty conscience
> and having our bodies washed with pure water. Let us
> hold unswervingly to the hope we profess, for he who
> promised is faithful. (Hebrews 10:19, 22-23)

Is it any surprise that near the end of the book of Revelation the rider of the white horse coming down from heaven, Jesus Christ Himself, is called "Faithful and True"

(19:11)? God is many things, but for those like me who have gone through the nightmare of the death of a spouse, God's faithfulness is so very comforting.

Just a little over two months before she died, Carol wrote me a good-bye letter. In fact, because she knew she was dying then, she wrote one for each of our four children as well. I want you to hear her words to me because, not only was she doing her best to prepare me for life without her, she was demonstrating remarkable faith in the faithfulness of God as she paused on the threshold of life's biggest change—death. Her absence of self-pity, her thankfulness, her humor and joy all point to a deep, deep faith.

May 27, 2006

Dearest Rob,

This is hard to write for so many reasons. The hardest reason, of course, is that I know if you're reading this then it means I am gone, and these are the last words I can leave with you. How can I possibly put on paper how much I love you and how much you mean to me? All the things that I love most about you are the qualities that have come out even stronger in the last nine months since I've been sick. Your protectiveness, your passion, and your faith—to name just a few. And I know they will carry you through the months and years ahead as you go on without me.

I also know that this letter finds you grieving, and I am not there, as I long to be, to comfort you.

*In fact—I am the cause of your grief—and that is
something that pains me terribly. And so what do I
say to you to lighten your burden and in some small
way to help you face the future?*

*First of all, you have been the best husband you
could possibly be to me. You should have <u>no regrets</u>,
Rob—you have been the world's best. You have loved
me in and through everything—from the thrill of our
honeymoon to the pain of cancer and death. We have
not been perfect, but we have stayed committed and
I believe God has honored that by giving us a great
love for each other. We have enjoyed so much together.
Raising children through those young years we thought
were so exhausting, only to find out that—yikes!—the
teenage years were even more difficult! Being surprised
by the joy of having a son when we thought three girls
were fine. (God knew back then that having Ryan
would be important during this time. If I didn't know
that you would have him at home with you, it would
make my leaving so much harder. But I know you will
be there for each other.) Think of our many romantic
vacations together, as well as our family times—you
have made all of those times so much fun because of
your zest for life and your love for us, and especially for
me. You have been faithful. I have never worried about
your faithfulness to me. You have been honest, you have
put our marriage first, and you have always made me
feel special and loved. I hope you always look back with*

a smile and with the knowledge that I considered it an honor and a privilege to be married to you.

Secondly, you <u>will</u> make it. I know there will be times you are overwhelmed, but God will see you through. He has not forsaken us through my illness, and He will not forsake you now. You have four children looking to you—and that will make the man in you rise up to care for them. You also have four children who will want to take care of <u>you</u> and comfort <u>you</u>—let them! They love you so much. They are <u>so</u> proud to have you as their dad. Give them lots of slack, especially the first year, and you will be fine. You don't have to be everything to all of them—let others take over at times. God didn't design you to be both father and mother—so just be the best dad you can be.

Which leads me to say, thirdly—that I give you my complete blessing to remarry. Not that you need me to say that, but I want to so that you know that I expect it and see it as healthy and positive. You are too amazing of a guy to keep away from others! You will need that outlet and need someone to love and be loved by. I always pictured us growing old together—but that is not to be. Instead, I will be ahead of you, cheering you on.

I have been amazed at how well you have handled all this. Sometimes I feel like I don't even know the real you—the deepest part of you that reaches out to God during this time and is touched by Him. God has given you an amazing ability to communicate those feelings and to be open about them at the right time. That time you spend with God is what makes you who you are; it's what gives you the depth that you have, and makes you the man others want to rely on. I have relied on you emotionally for much of our married life to bring us closer together spiritually, physically, and in so many other ways. It is the thing I most admire in you—your ability to be vulnerable and reveal yourself in a healthy way— not self-centered—but to show how God is working in your life. You are open about your struggles and feelings, while I am often so afraid of mine. Don't ever stop being who you are—because you are the most wonderful person I know. And hopefully I know you better than anybody! You are all man—yet with the ability to communicate deeply—from the heart. Which makes you an incredible pastor, preacher, husband, father, and friend. You give more to others than you'll ever know.

The real strength and measure of our marriage has not been that I am so lovable—but that <u>you</u> are so loving, and you are not afraid to show it. The most important thing to me is that I have always known that what you do will be based on your relationship with God—on what He wants from you—and not on your own wishes and desires. This has given me a deep trust in you, and in these last days, the knowledge that I am leaving the family in a good place. With you as their daddy—they can't go wrong! We will never be a perfect family, but I hope we are a godly one. As I face into *what the future has for me, I am so thankful that I have had you here by my side. I can never thank God enough for giving me you as a husband, when I didn't deserve you. I was not nearly at the place spiritually that you were, and yet somehow God brought us together and I am forever grateful. I love you so very much Rob. I hope I am able to pray for you all the more in heaven. I'm sorry for anything I've ever done to hurt you.*

All my love,

Carol

This letter helped me immensely through the darkness of my neutral zone. Each of Carol's letters to the five of us were blessings on the order of Old Testament blessings, painting a picture of our future, clarifying biblical priorities, and assuring us of God's faithfulness. But it was Carol's faith that was carrying her through her transition, making her radiance palpable to us all, and likewise, it would be our faith that would afford us the opportunity to transcend our coming wilderness experience, and whatever new beginnings lay ahead.

Our anchor in change is the Word of God

So change is painful and requires faith. A third truth about change is found in Joshua 1:7-8:

> Be strong and very courageous. Be careful to obey all
> the law my servant Moses gave you; do not turn from

it to the right or to the left, that you may be successful wherever you go. Do not let this Book of the Law depart from your mouth; meditate on it day and night, so that you may be careful to do everything written in it. Then you will be prosperous and successful.

The truth is this: our anchor in change is the Word of God. We overlook this truth at our peril. According to verse 7, our spiritual effectiveness is a function of our obedience to God. Then according to verse 8, our obedience is a function of our intake of God's Word. As a matter of fact, this verse couldn't be stated any stronger—it demands heavy lifting, or discipline, diligence, and persistence with God's Word. Note the language—"Do not let this Book of the Law depart from your mouth."

Sometimes people tell me they'd like to spend more time in God's Word but simply don't have room in their schedules. I tell them that busyness doesn't give them a pass; if anything, it makes this time that much more important. Remember that God was speaking to Joshua, the busiest man in Israel. His cup was overflowing with responsibilities—like a nation to oversee and an army to lead. Yet God called Joshua to a personal, continuous intake of God's Word. He commanded Joshua to stay connected. What a picture of the importance of the intake of God's Word!

Over and over I have told our church that it's not so much what you do in the moment of crisis that determines how you will come out of it, it's what you do in the months and years leading up to it.

For decades now, most days of the week, week in and week out, I get up and open my Bible and meditate on God's Word. Then I pray. From a human perspective, I am convinced that nothing I have ever done has been more important and helpful in preparing me for God's severe mercy. Nothing was more central to Carol; nothing was more catalytic for Tom.

In one of his e-mail updates, Tom quoted a verse he felt God had given him not long before. It became one of his favorite verses, and he frequently talked about it. The words had been written nearly two thousand years ago by the apostle Paul as he faced martyrdom:

> But I do not account my life of any value nor as
> precious to myself, if only I may finish my course
> and the ministry that I received from the Lord
> Jesus, to testify to the gospel of the grace of God.
> (Acts 20:24, ESV)

Tom added, "I feel so blessed to have God minister to me through His Word. I can't express my gratitude to Jesus, through Paul and the centuries of believers, many of whom gave their lives, that brought me my Bible."

We all have our weaknesses, tendencies toward pettiness, and blind spots, but as God lovingly revealed to Joshua, His Word can save us. Just like Carol and Tom, I love God's Word, and I long for you to love it as well.

Once when I preached on this subject, I went to one of my favorite psalms and quoted it from memory in its entirety. I wanted my church to see and to feel what God's Word means to me. People talked about the morning I quoted Psalm 103 for a while, mostly because they were sure I must have used notes.

But doesn't the psalmist affirm the empowering work of Scripture when he writes: "If your law had not been my delight, I would have perished in my affliction. I will never forget your precepts, for by them you have preserved my life" (Psalm 119:92-93)? And isn't this what the prophet Jeremiah illustrated centuries later, revealing the key to his thriving in the midst of Judah's darkest hour, when he says, "When your words came, I ate them; they were my joy and my heart's delight" (Jeremiah 15:16)? Isn't this why Paul thunders the familiar words, "All Scripture is God-breathed and is useful for teaching, rebuking, correcting and training in righteousness, so that the man of God may be thoroughly equipped for every good work" (2 Timothy 3:16-17)?

As author Francis Chan says, people who are obsessed with God are people who are obsessed with God's Word.[10] May Psalm 103, a portion of which follows, bless you as it has me. You should consider memorizing it too!

> Praise the LORD, O my soul;
>   all my inmost being, praise his holy name.
> Praise the LORD, O my soul,
>   and forget not all his benefits—
> who forgives all your sins
>   and heals all your diseases,

who redeems your life from the pit
and crowns you with love and compassion,
who satisfies your desires with good things
so that your youth is renewed like the eagle's.

The LORD works righteousness
and justice for all the oppressed.

He made known his ways to Moses,
his deeds to the people of Israel:
The LORD is compassionate and gracious,
slow to anger, abounding in love.

As we overcome deep disappointment and embark on a new beginning, we aren't simply undergoing a change from one specific set of circumstances to another. We are on a journey toward becoming increasingly like Jesus, a transition that leads to spiritual transformation. It's a much longer, deeper, and more painful journey than any of us would choose, yet it's exactly what our sovereign and faithful God decrees for His people. Again, disappointment isn't antithetical to the abundant life Jesus both promised and secured for us, it's central. The Bible tells us so.

Joy Opens the Door to New Beginnings

Before the Israelites entered the land promised to their forefather Abraham, they grieved the loss of what they saw as a familiar and secure life in Egypt. Then they had to navigate their way through the wilderness. Likewise, before embarking on a new beginning, you and I must grieve and transition from one set of circumstances to another. During our time in the wilderness, we may assume we will never again feel joy, never again feel delight just for being alive.

Yet, interestingly, God taught me nearly as much about joy as about sorrow during and after Carol's illness. I discovered that happiness apart from Jesus is fleeting; joy, however, is a natural outgrowth of our relationship with Christ. When He becomes the root, or Lord, of our life, joy is the fruit. We'll never get joy by seeking it first, but it's a by-product of seeking Christ above all. As C. S. Lewis puts it: "You can't get second things by putting them first. You get second things only by putting first things first."[11]

Joy is a second thing; Jesus is the first thing. When you and I embrace and submit to the lordship of Christ and do so together each and every day of our lives, ours will be joy now and forever. Joy is the visceral response to the reality, reign, and rule of the Lord Jesus Christ. Therefore, if we keep first things first, joy and pain aren't mutually exclusive, though we want them to be. God wants to mold us into the image of His Son, and often He uses something painful—an event that seemingly squashes joy—as a means to do that. Joy, therefore, isn't the absence of problems but the presence of Christ in the midst of them.

Never forget that the very same Jesus who promised His disciples "that my joy may be in you and that your joy may be complete" (John 15:11), also said to them "if anyone would come after me, he must deny himself and take up his cross and follow me" (Matthew 16:24). The cross, of course, was just about the most poignant metaphor for acute suffering in the first century. One of the great paradoxes of Kingdom living this side of heaven is that God molds and shapes His children by bringing things into our lives that, from our perspective, choke the very joy He wants to produce.

That's why Tom, in one of his e-mails, could point his family and friends to the life verse he'd adopted when he came to Christ three decades earlier: "He will not much remember the days of his life because God keeps him occupied with joy in his heart" (Ecclesiastes 5:20, ESV). More significant, that is why he could live—and die—with an attitude of joy. I believe that is also why Carol, in her final letter to me, could reflect with joy on all our family's blessings and add with hope, "I will be ahead of you, cheering you on."

Unexpected joy: My new beginning

Something strange happened several months after Carol's death. To my surprise, I learned that people at Wheaton Bible Church—a number of people, mostly independent of each other—were hoping and praying that God would enable Rhonda Williams and me to pick ourselves up from the ashes of our lives after losing our spouses. Specifically, they were praying that He might bring us together.

They were praying because they loved Rhonda and were worried about me. Suddenly, their pastor was a single parent with four kids. They didn't want me to fall apart or to take off to someplace like Southern California to hammer out a new life. Rhonda and I had had wonderful first marriages, so entering a new relationship wasn't what either of us expected. But with all those prayers, especially all the prayers of our elders' wives and other godly women, we didn't stand a chance.

On December 30, 2006, Rhonda and I went out to dinner with Jim, the chairman of our church's elder board, and his wife, Sandy. Nobody had any intention of starting anything between us that night. We were just getting together like we often did. But when Rhonda walked into the restaurant, I looked at her and saw her in a way I had never seen her before. I don't want to overspiritualize this, but at that moment, I clearly and distinctively thought, *Rob, how dumb do you have to be?* It was as if God was saying to me, *This is your future.*

Two days later, on New Year's Day, Rhonda and I, along with our families, went to watch football at Jim and Sandy's home. Getting together on New Year's was an annual tradition among my group of friends, but this year Rhonda and I spent a lot of time talking to one another. Frankly, we were beginning to feel something toward each other, something totally unanticipated but also totally undeniable. I sensed that Rhonda was one of a very small group of people who could understand what I was going through. Our common loss was like a magnet pulling us together.

That led to a series of very quiet, almost secretive, meetings. We would get together for lunch or go out for tea where we thought we wouldn't be seen by people who knew us. (It didn't work!) We were just trying to get to know each other on a different level, though Rhonda was stunned by all the things I knew about her. (That's because Tom and I had been accountability partners—Rhonda will have to take that up with Tom in heaven.) We also discussed what we were learning about grieving and how we were changing because of all we had been through. We were still bleeding, still off-center.

Over the course of just a couple of months, it became clear to me that I was falling in love all over again. It was strange. Carol and I had fallen in love quickly and were engaged four and a half months after we met and married just a little over six months later. Now the same thing was happening all over again, just as quickly—only this time I was nearing my midfifties with lots of miles under my hood; lots of wear on my tires.

Thirteen months after Carol's death and twenty-six months after Tom's, Rhonda and I became engaged. About four months later, just before Christmas 2007, we were married. And in this new beginning, God continues to shower us with His joy—and to transform us into the image of Christ.

CHAPTER 8

More Glimpses of Grace

THE GRIEF RHONDA AND I feel over the loss of our first spouses will never go away completely, but we echo Psalm 34:8: "Taste and see that the LORD is good." Believe me, God *has* been good.

Because our two families had been such good friends (Rhonda had been my son's pediatrician his entire life!), we find ourselves talking about Tom and Carol regularly as a new family. There are simply too many great stories, too many happy and shared memories, to shut off that season of our lives.

In this last chapter, I want to tell more of our story: the story of Rhonda, me, and our stepfamily. It's really the story of God's grace in the aftermath of two families' life-changing disappointment and loss. Cancer claimed our spouses, but we believe God gave us each other.

I wish I could say it's been a wonderful conclusion, super-easy, with a no-big-deal transition, but then I would be less than honest. Stepfamily life is fragile, complex, and full of ups and downs—way more so than anyone realizes on the front end. I write this chapter, in part, to face into that candidly, and also to encourage those of you in stepfamilies that you can navigate the minefields and overcome the difficulty and disappointment inherent in stepfamily living if you will look to Christ and walk by the Spirit.

From the beginning, our story did not play out like a fairy tale. On the one hand, we believed God might be leading us; on the other hand, it was strange for both of us because we had been such close family friends. Furthermore, as I mentioned in chapter 6, Rhonda felt that I had disappeared on her after Tom's death. When we started to see each other, she was still peeved at me. Fortunately, she told me so we could work through it. Boy, did I fall all over myself in apology and, boy, was Rhonda forgiving. Still, it wasn't the best way to start a relationship—all because after Tom went to be with Jesus, I went away as well.

I also didn't realize that Rhonda, like most women her age, was almost panicked by the thought of starting over with a new husband. In addition, she struggled over the notion of marrying a pastor—her pastor, no less—and the idea of taking on the role of pastor's wife. She understood what it was like to be married to a surgeon; but her uncertainty about the expectations she assumed came with being a pastor's wife led her to call off the whole thing at least two or three times. More than once she called me late at night and said, "Rob, I just can't do this."

As our relationship deepened, we began talking to our children about our dating. This was difficult. Our kids were still hurting, grieving, and raw. Now it appeared to them that we were abruptly and insensitively moving on. They expressed some confusion, some appropriate anger and hurt feelings. They also had lots of questions, everything from practical issues like "Where would we live?" to harder ones like "Will your remarriage mean your first marriages were less significant to God? Were they merely stepping-stones of sorts?"

The first question was relatively easy to navigate. We decided, based on good advice, not to move into each other's homes—not to have Rhonda try to live in "Carol's house" or me in "Tom's house." Certainly we didn't want to put any of our seven kids into this situation, so we ended up buying a different house.

Our kids' second question also deserved an answer. My response wasn't to necessarily disagree; Rhonda and I were moving things along quickly and it did appear that we were being insensitive. Rhonda and I understood that. After acknowledging their feelings, however, I went on to add a couple of other things: First, in no way were we attempting to deny anyone's grieving or for that matter legislate how anyone needed to feel about the timing of our relationship. Second, I explained that I felt this was an unusual set of circumstances and that maybe God was doing something we didn't expect. Third and most important, I clarified that our relationship was not about dishonoring Tom or Carol. They were fantastic people, and we would always work hard to keep their memories alive. Actually, because we knew them so well, we felt our relationship would honor their memories.

We were married in a small, relatively informal ceremony on a Sunday afternoon, December 16, 2007, with all our kids and close friends present. In fact, our seven kids served as our wedding party and were unusually supportive.

To visualize our story and honor our former spouses, Rhonda chose a wedding ring with three stones—two smaller stones and a larger center one. The two smaller stones symbolize our previous marriages. The larger stone is a symbol of our new stepfamily.

There were some twists that made the day especially memorable. For starters, Rhonda's mother, whom she considers her best friend, was unable to attend because she had just had emergency open-heart surgery. On the morning of our wedding, my stepfather of thirty-one years died out of state at age ninety-one. Then that evening, the first night of our honeymoon, my kids went back to our house and started a fire in the fireplace. We've had fires on many cold winter nights, but this time the chimney caught on fire! The kids, however, couldn't see the fire spewing out of the chimney outside. Fortunately, our neighbors did, and they called the fire department. Not long after, several firemen, all with very serious looks on their faces, stormed into our house to put out the fire. We will never forget that day.

Rhonda and I are busy at work and busy at home but we relish our time together. We share a lot of common interests. We love traveling, working in the yard, biking, and going to dinner and a movie together. Rhonda works hard to bring our large family together for birthdays and holidays, and she almost exhausts herself making sure everyone is treated fairly.

I love her sense of humor and the priority she places on family, but I have been especially encouraged by her love for our church. She has been a great pastor's wife despite her busy medical practice. Recently, when we were in Israel, I was serving Communion in the Garden Tomb and looked over and saw this strong, dear woman weeping, overcome by the wonder of Christ's death for our sins. Our shared tragedies and our profoundly personal awareness of the fragility of life have knit our hearts together in ways you'd have to experience to completely understand. But the truth is, our new marriage and new stepfamily has been one huge adjustment and, to be completely honest, terribly disappointing at times.

Yes, we are deeply in love, deeply enjoying each other, but I am very different from Tom and Rhonda is different from Carol. Tom and Carol were the two more laid-back temperaments in our marriages. They were both easygoing peacemakers. Rhonda and I, however, are both type A controllers, bossy, more uptight. We do not like to be controlled, and we both spend our days telling a fair number of people what to do.

A friend of ours, who is also a highly esteemed counselor, gave us a great warning early in our relationship: "When you guys argue, you will really argue. That's not necessarily all bad, but just be really careful, or it will be!" He was absolutely right.

For example, I will never forget a time when we were dating and discussing a sensitive subject somewhat heatedly. Rhonda looked at me and said, "Tom would never talk to me like that!" I wasn't in the best mood at the moment (that's a slight understatement), but I considered her words. Then I thought about my friend Tom and how easy and calming he was to be with. I started laughing out loud and said, "You are absolutely right. Tom probably wouldn't respond like this. He would say 'whatever' and move on!"

We've had to make other adjustments as well. I am a communicator and like to talk. I am also fairly subjective, fairly sensitive, and have always enjoyed discussing feelings in a fair amount of detail. That's especially true late at night when I should be sleeping but can't. Rhonda, however, is much more objective, much less concerned about analyzing feelings (she's a trained physician who excelled at organic chemistry), and when she comes home at the end of a day after seeing thirty to forty patients, she isn't usually up for a whole lot of in-depth conversation, especially late at night.

Not long ago, though, I got some helpful practice at speaking less. My stepdaughter Kelly, a middle-school teacher in inner-city Los Angeles, married Jared, who is on staff with Fellowship of Christian Athletes in Orange County. Because they live so far away and were getting married back here in Chicago where they both grew up, a lot of the details fell on Rhonda. One Sunday I joked with the congregation that the role of the father of the bride is precarious, but the role of the stepfather is treacherous.

I walked Kelly down the aisle at her request and also performed the ceremony, so all was really good on that front. Still, I learned along the way—you stepfathers listen to me—when it comes to a stepfamily wedding like this, two things are essential: (1) don't speak unless you are asked, and (2) when asked, don't speak! Stay silent. Don't complain. By the way, I got about a C plus on this.

Holidays have been another stressor. Our first couple of Christmases as a stepfamily just about did Rhonda in (not to mention the children) as she tried to honor different family traditions involving meals, decorations, opening presents, and the like. It's amazing what traditionalists we all become around Christmas, regardless of age. The Williams family, for example, opened presents on Christmas Eve and always had Norwegian meatballs to eat for dinner. The Bugh family, on the other hand, had to work around my busy church schedule, so we never opened presents on Christmas Eve and always had a steak dinner, which we ate really fast before dashing back to church. And that was just Christmas Eve!

After a couple of years of stepfamily craziness, Rhonda asked a couple of the kids if they thought we could start a few of our own new traditions and then asked them to give her their input. This worked really well for us, and Rhonda finally was able to enjoy a stepfamily Christmas.

In his wonderful but sobering book *The Smart Stepfamily*, author Ron Deal says the best metaphor for a stepfamily isn't a blended family. That image suggests that you throw all the ingredients into a blender, stir it up, and everything comes out the same and everyone feels the same. A better metaphor for a stepfamily, he says, is a Crock-Pot. Why? Two different families bring lots of different personalities, so forming a stepfamily is like putting meat, potatoes, and a variety of vegetables into the pot. The pot, in our case, is Rhonda and Rob; the kids are the other ingredients. A Crock-Pot cooks over a long period of time at low heat. As it does, the carrots stay carrots and the beef remains beef. And that is a great picture of what it takes to have a smart or successful stepfamily—lots of time and low heat, which translates into generous portions of sensitivity. Family members should not be pressured to grieve or conform or even engage in a certain way. In addition, it should be made clear that some things will never, ever morph into the tidy package that intact or biological families experience.

Ron Deal suggests it takes successful stepfamilies up to seven years to really gain traction and positive family momentum. Because he focuses full-time on the stepfamily and the church, Ron has been a big help, not only to Rhonda and me, but to our small group, which is composed of other couples who have formed stepfamilies. I know there are differences of opinion on the biblical grounds for divorce and remarriage and that a stepfamily like ours that came together following the death of two spouses is more the exception than the norm. Regardless, stepfamilies are all around us, and I personally think every church should have a support group or groups for stepfamilies, to help them grapple with their very difficult and complex world. There is hope, as Ron so clearly offers:

> There is a honeymoon for couples in stepfamilies, it just comes at the end of the journey and not at the beginning. Ongoing research of couples in stepfamilies . . . confirms that couples in stepfamilies can create high quality marital relationships. . . . As with all marriages—whether a first or fifth—qualities like effective communication, the ability to resolve conflict well, a relational style that is flexible and adaptable, enjoying leisure activities together, and couple spirituality prove to be very predictive of a high quality marital relationship. . . .
>
> In other words, couples can create mutually satisfying, intimate, God-honoring marriages within stepfamilies. Undoubtedly, there are a number of unique barriers to overcome . . . but remarriages can be healthy relationships. Furthermore, I've observed that couples that endure the adversity of the journey frequently have a bond that is powerful enough to withstand anything. There is strength and a sense of victory after surviving what for some is a difficult journey.

And how long does it take for couples to find an increase of satisfaction? E. Mavis Hetherington reports, in her highly scientific book *For Better or For Worse: Divorce Reconsidered*, that it takes most couples five to seven years to get through the tensions of stepfamily life, such that their stress level declines to match that of a husband and wife in a first marriage. Furthermore, surviving their tumultuous early years seems to give couples a staying power that keeps them going . . . and growing.[1]

Rhonda and I are learning to give our kids, who have been unusually supportive, space and time. In addition, we are attempting to be realistic about our own personal expectations for our marriage and for our children. We believe that in the aftermath of great loss, God is weaving us together by His grace and for His glory, even in and through our grief.

Our experience has confirmed that God's grace is sufficient; frankly, I do not know how people who do not know Christ do any of this in their own power, nor am I surprised that the divorce rate among remarriages is so high. I, for one, would have quickly drowned in the sea of my own sorrow, self-pity, and self-centeredness! But in Christ, "I can do everything through him who gives me strength" (Philippians 4:13). Trust me, at 2 a.m. after you have been sobbing for what seems like hours, those, dear friends, aren't just ancient words. Those words are a divine lifeline, connecting us to the One who loves us so much He died to rescue us from ourselves!

Ultimately we are convinced that what will sustain us is the same thing that enabled us to get through the massive disappointment that followed the cancer diagnoses and the deaths of our first spouses: passionate prayer, both by ourselves and from others. Never again will we underestimate the power of prayer, the power of a praying church. In his book *Your God Is Too Safe*, Mark Buchanan includes a story I used over and over and then, to my utter surprise, a story I experienced personally in my greatest disappointment. He writes:

> William Willimon tells another story. A man he knew went to Russia in the late seventies, at the height of the Cold War. He was sent as part of a delegation from the World Council of Churches to investigate and report on the state of the Christian church under an atheist regime. The man was not impressed.
>
> "The church," he told Willimon dismissively, contemptuously, "is just a bunch of little old ladies praying." . . .
>
> Willimon told that story in the early nineties, when statues of Stalin and Lenin—the patron saints of atheistic Russia—lay toppled, ready to be crated for storage or quarried for stone.

Beware little old ladies praying. Secretly they're revolutionaries who make Bolsheviks look like kindergartners. They comprise a veritable bomb-making factory.

Pray the Psalms—offer your whole life before God. Pray without ceasing—bring your whole life into the presence of God.

For now it's incense.

But one day, in the hands of the God who is not safe but good, the fire will fall, and everything will become as it was meant to be.[2]

Beware of a mother, a young child, a coworker praying. But especially, beware of a church that prays! Rhonda and I have experienced the power of specific, impassioned prayer, and we are forever grateful.

Prayer is the lifeline that keeps us intimately connected to God before, during, and after life's greatest disappointments. Even when the bottom drops out, we can rest in the knowledge that God will never forsake us and that He stands ready to pour His grace, mercy, and peace into our lives if we will surrender and believe.

Our wedding day
December 16, 2007

Discussion

3. Have yo
your

INTRODUCTION

1. What is your response to the question with which
   Rob opens the book: "Have you ever tried to convince
   yourself that if you believe enough and are godly
   enough, good things will happen—and if they do not,
   you'd better not let on so you don't appear less than
   spiritual?" (p. xi). Explain.

2. Why do you think people—especially Christians—
   sometimes have difficulty being open about their
   struggles?

u ever experienced the bottom dropping out of
own life? If so, what did that look like for you?

4. According to Rob, what are the consequences
   of denying your pain? Can you think of other
   potential consequences? If so, what are they?

5. We know loss can be horrific. Why, then, does God
   permit pain in our lives? Why is it important to
   accept both adversity and God's sovereignty in it?

CHAPTER 1: INTO THE DEPTHS

1. How would you describe the ways in which Tom and Carol each enriched Rob's life?

2. In his first e-mail to family and friends after he was diagnosed with cancer, Tom wrote: "I wonder if God has been preparing me for 50 years to handle this." Based on what you now know about his life, in what ways would you say God prepared him for his illness?

3. Second Corinthians 1:9-11. reads:

   Indeed, in our hearts we felt the sentence of death. But this happened that we might not rely on ourselves but on God, who raises the dead. He has delivered us from such a deadly peril, and he will deliver us. On him we have set our hope that he will continue to deliver us, as you help us by your prayers. Then many will give thanks on our behalf for the gracious favor granted us in answer to the prayers of many.

Why do you think this became such a meaningful passage to Tom? In what way does this passage speak to you today?

4. Carol found the following quote from Eugene Peterson's book *A Long Obedience in the Same Direction* quite meaningful in her own struggle with significance:

> The only serious mistake we can make when illness comes, when anxiety threatens, when conflict disturbs our relationships with others is to conclude that God has gotten bored in looking after us and has shifted his attention to a more exciting Christian, or that God has become disgusted with our meandering obedience and decided to let us fend for ourselves for a while, or that God has gotten too busy fulfilling prophecy in the Middle

East to take time now to sort out the complicated mess we have gotten ourselves into.

Does any part of Peterson's quote resonate with you? If so, how?

5. As he assumed leadership of the Israelites from Moses, Joshua was told: "The LORD himself goes before you and will be with you; he will never leave you nor forsake you. Do not be afraid; do not be discouraged" (Deuteronomy 31:8). What are some of the ways Rob and Carol realized God was going ahead of them in their battle? Describe an experience in which you've seen evidence that God was going with you or someone else through a time of trouble.

6. What is the difference between Christ followers who seem to transcend their circumstances and those who do not?

7. Rob notes that navigating great trouble in God's strength inevitably leads to transformation. In what way was Rob changed through the illnesses and deaths of Tom and Carol? In what way would you say that God transformed you during a time of great difficulty in your own life?

CHAPTER 2: TRUTHS IN THE NIGHT

1. Have you ever had a "laundry room moment" like Rob's? Explain.

2. Do you agree that "too many of us expect too much out of life" (p. 29)? Why or why not? What does Scripture (e.g., Romans 5:12; 8:18-22) have to say about this?

3. Do you agree that "denying the existence of God doesn't make disappointment and tragedy any easier" (p. 35)? Why or why not?

4. Central to resting in God's sovereignty, writes Rob, is submission. As you read this chapter, did you find yourself relating most to the experiences of Joseph, Job, or Jesus when it comes to learning to submit to the heavenly Father? Explain.

5. The New Testament word for submission is *hupo-tasso*, a Greek compound word meaning to "place oneself under." What area of your life would you say is most in need of being placed under God?

6. Jim Harrell once said, "We truly don't see God and his purpose and strength without suffering, because we just become too comfortable" (p. 46). Do you agree or disagree? Why?

7. Has your view of heaven changed as a result of painful circumstances you've lived through? If so, how?

8. What does Rob mean when he says, "What soap is to the hands, suffering is to the soul" (p. 48)?

CHAPTER 3: SEEING GOD ABOVE ALL, OVER ALL, IN ALL . . . JOSEPH

1. Drawing on examples from this chapter or from your own life, describe someone who handled adversity well. Then describe someone who seemed to drown in hopelessness as a result of suffering. Do you agree with Rob that people's view of God makes the difference in their response? Explain.

2. What enabled Tom to face his diagnosis with hope and thanksgiving? How did his outlook differ from mere positive thinking?

3. In what two ways does Rob define virtue? What is virtue's connection to the way we handle disappointment?

4. Describe a time when you found yourself underestimating God's power.

5. From the world's perspective, it might have appeared expedient for Joseph to act on the advances of Potiphar's wife or for Shadrach, Meshach, and Abednego to bow down and pretend to worship a statue. Why did they refuse to compromise? What enabled them to do so?

6. Why do we so often resist what God has allowed into our lives? What are the benefits of resting in the sovereignty of God?

7. Would you say you're most in need of learning to trust in God's holiness, power, or sovereignty? Name one way that following Joseph's example could help you do that.

CHAPTER 4: TURNING ADVERSITY INTO ADVANTAGE . . . ABRAHAM

1. In his book on prayer, Philip Yancey describes two kinds of faith: (1) bold, childlike trust and (2) fidelity faith. What are the similarities? What are the differences?

2. What do you think it means to "get stuck on the back side of a question mark" (p. 90)? Why is that a dangerous place to remain?

3. Is it wrong to ask questions and seek answers during adversity? Give an example of when it is appropriate to do so. Give an example when it is counterproductive to demand answers.

4. Have you ever suspected that God has forgotten about you? Explain.

5. British pastor Martyn Lloyd-Jones cautions that listening to yourself can lead to spiritual depression. Do you agree? What is the solution?

6. What does Rob mean when he points out that life is often "messy in the middle" (p. 98)? Can you think of a person or a situation that demonstrates the truth of that statement? If so, explain.

7. Why does Rob say that sacrificing for God leads to a life of meaning and contentment? Do you agree? If so, give an example of someone who demonstrates this truth. If you disagree, explain why.

CHAPTER 5: PERSEVERING FAITH . . . JEREMIAH

1. What family member, friend, or historical figure would you point to as a great model of persevering faith? Why?

2. What does Jeremiah teach us about persevering faith?

3. Explain the cause-and-effect relationship between faith and perseverance.

4. What characteristics of God can give us hope, even during the most desperate of situations?

5. Jeremiah wrote: "The LORD is good to those whose hope is in him, to the one who seeks him" (Lamentations 3:25). According to Jeremiah, how do we put ourselves in a position to see the goodness of God? Can you relate a time when you found this principle to be true?

6. We see David's passion for God summed up in Psalm 63:1, which reads: "O God, you are my God, earnestly I seek you; my soul thirsts for you, my body longs for you, in a dry and weary land where there is no water." How well does this psalm express your own feelings for God right now? Whether you resonate with David's deep dependence on God or are currently battling anger and disappointment with Him, write your own thoughts (perhaps even in the form of a psalm) to God.

7. What is the value of silence as we seek to submit ourselves to God?

8. Perseverance is possible when we are (1) clear about God's character, (2) dependent on His faithfulness, (3) passionate about our relationship with Him, (4) completely submitted to His plan, and (5) committed to obey Him. In which of these five areas

do you most want to grow? What is one step you could take immediately to begin developing in that area?

CHAPTER 6: GOOD GRIEF

1. Do you agree that grief is an inevitable by-product of a major loss? Why or why not?

2. Why do so many people try to avoid grief? What are some of the possible results of doing so?

3. Rob points out that grief is inevitable, profound, and disorienting. If you have suffered a significant loss in your life, what else did you learn about grief?

4. If you have ever grieved a major loss, describe something someone did for you that was particularly comforting.

5. Rob admits that, as a pastor, he once tried to come up with nuggets of wisdom to pass on to grieving people. As you think about the ways you have responded to a grieving friend or loved one, can you see anything you wish you'd done differently?

6. Rob admits that he once thought God might be speaking directly to his situation through Scripture, only to discover that he was mistaken. What can we learn from his experience?

7. Think of a grieving friend, family or church member, coworker, or neighbor. Now review the partial list of God's promises on pages 161–162. Which of these assurances—or perhaps another promise from Scripture—would you say that person most needs to hear? How can you best communicate that truth to him or her?

CHAPTER 7: THE CHALLENGE OF CHANGE

1. The reality of his family's situation hit Rob particularly hard one night while he was getting ready for bed in a hotel room far from home. Can you recall a similar moment in your own life? If so, describe.

2. Why do you think Rob is careful to point out that, while we need to embrace many types of change, we should not open ourselves to theological change?

3. Why did God repeatedly tell the Israelites to "be strong and courageous" as they prepared to enter the Promised Land? What is the takeaway for us today?

4. How would you explain the distinction between transition and change? Do you agree it is important to understand the difference? Why or why not?

5. According to William Bridges, psychological transition involves three steps: (1) the ending, losing, letting go; (2) the neutral zone; and (3) the new beginning. As you consider Rob's story or a change you're undergoing in your own life, explain which circumstances fit into each category.

6. Do you agree that navigating change effectively requires faith? Why or why not?

7. As you read the letter Carol wrote to Rob, what struck you most? How does the letter illustrate that Carol was working through her own transition?

8. Why do you think Rob considers spending time in God's Word so critical to getting through change?

9. Rob explains how the greatest loss of his life was unexpectedly followed by joy. Can you tell of a time when deep pain was followed by joy in your own life?

CHAPTER 8: MORE GLIMPSES OF GRACE

1. In what ways do you think the close preexisting bond between their families helped Rob and Rhonda as they began to date? How did it make their relationship more difficult?

2. Ron Deal says, "There is a honeymoon for couples in stepfamilies, it just comes at the end of the journey and not at the beginning" (p. 207). Do you think Rob and Rhonda's experiences as a couple confirm this? Why or why not?

3. Why do you think Rob ends his book by telling a story about the power of prayer?

4. How has this book changed your understanding of loss and disappointment?

5. Do you think you'll handle disappointment any differently after reading this book? If so, explain.

Endnotes

CHAPTER 1: INTO THE DEPTHS

1. Eugene Peterson, *A Long Obedience in the Same Direction* (Downers Grove, IL: InterVarsity Press, 1980), 38–39.

CHAPTER 2: TRUTHS IN THE NIGHT

1. Cornelius Plantinga, *Not the Way It's Supposed to Be: A Breviary of Sin* (Grand Rapids, MI: Wm. B. Eerdmans, 1995).
2. Wayne Grudem, *Systematic Theology* (Grand Rapids, MI: Zondervan, 1994), 495.
3. Ibid.
4. Douglas Moo, *The Epistle to the Romans* (Grand Rapids, MI: Wm. B. Eerdmans, 1996), 516.
5. GoJerusalem.com, "The History of the American Colony Hotel Part One—From Chicago to Jerusalem—1871 to 1881," http://www .gojerusalem.com/article_1383/The-History-of-the-American-Colony -Hotel-Part-One---From-Chicago-to-Jerusalem---1871-to-1881.
6. Joni Eareckson Tada and Steven Estes, *When God Weeps* (Grand Rapids, MI: Zondervan, 1997), 84.
7. James Means, *A Tearful Celebration* (Sisters, OR: Multnomah, 1984), 37.
8. Randy Alcorn, "Jim Harrell, Perspectives in Suffering, Part 3," *The Eternal Perspectives Blog*, December 11, 2008, http://www.epm.org/blog/2008 /Dec/11/jim-harrell-perspectives-in-suffering-part-3.
9. Rob Moll, *The Art of Dying* (Downers Grove, IL: InterVarsity Press, 2010), 83.
10. Randy Alcorn, *If God Is Good: Faith in the Midst of Suffering and Evil* (Colorado Springs, CO: Multnomah Books, 2009), 420.

11. Paul E. Billheimer, *Don't Waste Your Sorrows: Finding God's Purpose in the Midst of Pain* (Minneapolis: Bethany House, 1977), 62.
12. Randy Alcorn, *Heaven* (Carol Stream, IL: Tyndale House, 2004), 359–360.
13. Michael Horton, *Christless Christianity: The Alternative Gospel of the American Church* (Grand Rapids, MI: Baker, 2008), 132.
14. Tim Keller, *The Reason for God: Belief in an Age of Skepticism* (New York: Penguin Group, 2008), 30–31.
15. J. C. Ryle, *Holiness: Its Nature, Difficulties, Hindrances, and Roots* (Chicago, IL: Moody Publishers, 2010), 222.

CHAPTER 3: SEEING GOD ABOVE ALL, OVER ALL, IN ALL . . . JOSEPH
1. We know Joseph's approximate age here because just two chapters earlier in Genesis 37:2, we are told that Joseph was seventeen, and "soon after this" (37:12, NLT) he was sold into slavery.
2. I highly recommend Tom's book: *Breakthrough: The Return of Hope to the Middle East* (Colorado Springs, CO: Authentic, 2008).
3. Gary Haugen, *Just Courage: God's Great Expedition for the Restless Christian* (Downers Grove, IL: InterVarsity Press, 2008), 31–32.
4. Philip Yancey, *What's So Amazing about Grace?* (Grand Rapids, MI: Zondervan, 1997), 85.
5. Tony Snow, "Cancer's Unexpected Blessings," *Christianity Today*, July 20, 2007.

CHAPTER 4: TURNING ADVERSITY INTO ADVANTAGE . . . ABRAHAM
1. Paul G. Stoltz and Erik Weihenmayer, *The Adversity Advantage* (New York: Fireside, 2010), xvi.
2. David Platt, *Radical: Taking Back Your Faith from the American Dream* (Colorado Springs, CO: Multnomah, 2010), 71.
3. Philip Yancey, *Prayer: Does It Make Any Difference?* (Grand Rapids, MI: Zondervan, 2006), 278.
4. Ibid., 196–197.
5. Ibid., 197.
6. John R. Rice, *742 Heart-Warming Poems* (Murfreesboro, TN: Sword of the Lord, 1982), 18.
7. We know these details from Genesis 17:1, 17 and from Romans 4:18-19, where Paul tells us, "Against all hope, Abraham in hope believed and so became the father of many nations. . . . Without weakening in his faith, he faced the fact that his body was as good as dead—since his body was about a hundred years old—and that Sarah's womb was also dead."
8. Yancey, *Prayer*, 211–212.

CHAPTER 5: PERSEVERING FAITH . . . JEREMIAH

1. In her book *The River of Doubt* (New York: Doubleday, 2005), Candice Millard brings this harrowing adventure—as well as the river route the explorers followed—to life.
2. John and Alice Durant, *Pictorial History of American Presidents* (New York: A. S. Barnes & Co., 1955), 114.
3. Gary Thomas, *Sacred Marriage* (Grand Rapids, MI: Zondervan, 2000), 135.
4. Ibid.
5. Ibid., 136.
6. Ibid., 136–138.
7. A similar diagram appears in Bruce Wilkinson and Kenneth Boa, *Talk Thru the Bible* (Nashville, TN: Thomas Nelson, 1983), 209.
8. "Faith Matters for Kristin Armstrong," interview with Michel Martin, National Public Radio, May 11, 2007, http://www.npr.org/templates /story/story.php?storyId=10132951.
9. *The 700 Club*, "Live Stronger: Kristin Armstrong's Divorce Recovery Journey," http://www.cbn.com/700club/guests/bios/Kristin _Armstrong033007.aspx.
10. If, like me, you struggle in this area, I also recommend memorizing Proverbs 13:3 and 17:27.
11. Snow, "Cancer's Unexpected Blessings."

CHAPTER 6: GOOD GRIEF

1. Raymond R. Mitsch and Lynn Brookside, *Grieving the Loss of Someone You Love* (Ventura, CA: Regal, 1993), 89–90.
2. Scott Campbell and Phyllis Silverman, *Widower: When Men Are Left Alone* (Amityville, NY: Baywood Publishing, 1996), 226.
3. Ibid., 17.
4. Ibid., 18.
5. Alcorn, *If God Is Good*, 382.
6. Horton, *Christless Christianity*, 21, 68.
7. Ibid., 69.
8. Ibid., 80.
9. Alcorn, *If God Is Good*, 382–383.

CHAPTER 7: THE CHALLENGE OF CHANGE

1. G. K. Chesterton, *Orthodoxy* (Nashville, TN: Sam Torode Book Arts, 2009), 27.
2. If this is a topic with which you want to grapple further, I recommend Kevin DeYoung and Ted Kluck's book *Why We're Not Emergent: By Two*

Guys Who Should Be (Chicago: Moody Publishers, 2008). This book has led to a lot of positive discussion among the ministry staff at Wheaton Bible Church.

3. William Bridges, *Managing Transitions: Making the Most of Change* (New York, NY: Perseus Books, 1991), 3–4.
4. Ibid., 4–5.
5. Ibid., 8.
6. The chart depicting this process has been adapted from Bridges, *Managing Transitions*, 5.
7. Ibid., 39 (quoting Marilyn Ferguson).
8. William Shakespeare, *Othello* (Act II, scene iii, lines 376–377), quoted by Bridges, *Managing Transitions*, 140.
9. Bridges, *Managing Transitions*, 9.
10. Francis Chan, *Crazy Love: Overwhelmed by a Relentless God* (Colorado Springs, CO: David C. Cook, 2008), 143.
11. C. S. Lewis, "First and Second Things," in *God in the Dock: Essays on Theology and Ethics* (Grand Rapids, MI: Wm. B. Eerdmans, 1994), 280.

CHAPTER 8: MORE GLIMPSES OF GRACE
1. Ron Deal, *The Smart Stepfamily* (Bloomington, MN: Bethany House, 2002), 25–26.
2. Mark Buchanan, *Your God Is Too Safe* (Sisters, OR: Multnomah, 2001), 235.